Milly.

Cues

Act 1 - 13
  , 2 - 7
  , 3 - 20
          40

FIND THE TIGER

A Thriller in Three Acts for Women

By PATRICIA BROOKS

PRICE 5s. NET

London:
H. F. W. DEANE & SONS LTD.
31 MUSEUM STREET, W.C.1
BOSTON, MASS., U.S.A.: THE WALTER H. BAKER COMPANY
MADE IN ENGLAND

ACTING FEES FOR PERFORMANCES OVERSEAS

Apply—South Africa: Darter & Sons, Cape Town. Kenya: National Theatre, P.O. Box 482, Nairobi. Southern and Northern Rhodesia: Federal Theatre League, Private Box 167H, Salisbury. Australia: Doreen Rayment, Flat 17, 229 Miller Street, North Sydney. New Zealand: John Bush Play Bureau, P.O. Box 273, Hawera. Canada and U.S.A.: The Walter H. Baker Company, Boston.

CHARACTERS:

MISS EMILIA DALE—*Principal and Matron of Randiddles Home, a health clinic in Sussex. Aged about 48, she is an upright, stiff woman of firm character.*

SUSAN LINDY—*Niece of Miss Dale. A pretty, pleasant-looking girl of 28. She has been secretary to her aunt for many years.*

VICTORIA PENROSE—*Is known as "Viccy". She is the chief beauty counsellor and has an extremely smart hair-style. She wears either well-cut slacks with a shirt blouse, or a smart nylon overall, with high-heeled shoes.*

MILLY TIPTON—*A rather dour "treasure" of a maid who has been with Miss Dale for many years. She wears a blue overall, and is aged about 55.*

GUESTS AT THE CLINIC:

ERICA HESTON—*A rather hard-faced woman of about 50. She dresses in a plain suit or dress and has a harsh, slightly common voice.*

LADY COULSDEN—*A very old lady, slightly deaf and rather vague. Her dresses are long and fussy. She peers over her spectacles.*

MRS. RUTH STACEY-BROWN—*Is a rich, cheerful, plump woman of about 45. Her dress is a little too youthful for her and her voice has a very slightly common tone.*

MISS CLARA FANTON—*Can be almost any age between 30 and 50. Ideally, she should be thin and rather badly dressed, in tweedy clothes.*

MRS. RONA WINSTONE—*A slim, pretty woman of about 35. Her dresses are very smart, but plain and severe. An obvious "county" type.*

MISS TESSA TREVALLION, or MRS. DARKE—*A smart, sophisticated woman, rather heavily made-up. She is an actress and speaks with a slight drawl. She admits to 25 but is probably over 30.*

SCENE:

RANDIDDLES HOUSE—*Health clinic in Sussex. The room, which is used as an office, is pleasant, but slightly shabby. The door, which opens to the hall, is U.L. There is a window, underneath which is a window seat, C.B. A fireplace is C.L.*

A large desk, aslant, D.R., holds a telephone, typewriter, lamp, numerous ledgers and papers. Behind it is a small chair. A tall cupboard or filing cabinet is right of the window and, left, a low bookcase on which stands a fine arrangement of flowers. A table on the right wall can hold another lamp or ornament, but room must be left upon it to hold a coffee-tray. There is a settee, C.R., across the stage, with a low coffee-table near it, though this can be dispensed with if necessary. A tall-backed armchair is upstage near fireplace, and another small armchair downstage. A chair is backstage, near the filing cabinet. Cigarettes are in a box on mantelpiece, also on desk.

These instructions are from the audience point of view.

Christian names are used for the sake of brevity.

FIND THE TIGER

A THRILLER IN THREE ACTS FOR WOMEN
By PATRICIA BROOKS

ACT I.

Early afternoon.

When the curtain goes up the stage is empty but almost immediately the door opens and MRS. RUTH STACEY-BROWN *peers cautiously around it. Seeing that the room is empty, she closes the door carefully, walks to settee, and drops on it with an audible sigh of relief. She kicks off her shoes, swings up her feet, and, leaning back comfortably, closes her eyes. There is a pause and then the door opens and* MISS CLARA FANTON *looks in. Seeing Ruth, she, too, closes the door carefully and tiptoes over to the settee. Then in a loud, stern voice, meant to imitate Matron, she speaks:*

CLARA. Mrs. Stacey-Brown, what are you doing in this office so early in the afternoon?

(RUTH *almost falls off the settee in surprise.*)

RUTH. Gosh! You wretch! You almost gave me a heart attack.

CLARA. Ah! Guilty conscience! What *are* you doing hiding in Susan's office so early in the afternoon? You've finished very early.

RUTH. Not finished, I just ducked out. Viccy thinks I'm with Gloria and Gloria thinks Viccy has me. (*She laughs.*)

CLARA (*chair, fireplace*). Isn't that a little dishonest?

RUTH (*cheerfully*). I expect so, but after a fortnight of this place I'm past caring. Do you know what Viccy had me doing yesterday?

CLARA. What?

RUTH. I had to lie flat on my back and pick up a marble somewhere near my left shoulder with my feet. I ask you!

CLARA. A physical impossibility, I should say.

RUTH. Oh, no! Viccy can do it, but I rolled about until I was sea-sick. Can you see me doing a trick like that?

CLARA (*taking a cigarette from mantelpiece*). What, may I ask, was supposed to be the result of all these gymnastics?

RUTH. Oh! Hip reduction, or something, but it didn't do a thing for me. Viccy threatened me with another dose today, so I dodged.

CLARA. So, I think, should I. But if you—er—dodge, aren't you rather wasting time and money?

RUTH (*cheerfully*). I've got wads of both, dearie, and there's some things I'm prepared to do for the Body Bee-u-tiful that they talk so much about, and some I'm not.

CLARA. I see. You have a selective mind.

RUTH. No, dear, I've practically no mind at all, but I know what I can do and what *I* can't. Have you seen poor old Lady Coulsden? They've got her properly frizzled.

CLARA. Surely she doesn't do exercises? She must be over seventy!

RUTH. She does! True, they call them "gentle relaxation", but what Viccy calls "gentle" would run a sergeant-major into the ground in a couple of days.

CLARA. Then why does she come here? After all, this treatment is quite expensive and you could call very little of it enjoyable.

RUTH. She's just dumped, the poor old trotty.

CLARA. Dumped? What do you mean?

RUTH. She lives with a couple of dim relatives and each year, when they want to go on holiday, they just dump her here.

CLARA. I see!

RUTH. Personally, I think they're trying to give her a gentle push.

CLARA. That statement sounds slightly slanderous to me.

RUTH (*laughs*). Perhaps it is, but I think she enjoys it in a way, because she likes meeting new people so that she can tell them how she was once "Her Excellency in Boona"—or Poona—or somewhere.

CLARA. Was she, indeed? How interesting!

RUTH. Have you met the two new "girls"?

CLARA. No. When did they arrive?

RUTH. One of them arrived after dinner last night and hasn't been seen since.

CLARA. What have they done with the body?

RUTH (*laughs*). I gathered from Susan that Matron is furious. You know how she likes to "receive" everyone.

CLARA. Yes. A half-hour's inquisition and a glass of bad sherry in her "sanctum".

RUTH. Here! I didn't even get the sherry! I bin robbed!

CLARA. You were favoured, I should say.

RUTH (*laughs again*). Well, I gather that this bod sweeps up to her room and announces that she will "interview" Matron tomorrow.

CLARA. Did she, indeed? I'm looking forward to meeting *her*.

RUTH. So Matron has been biting her nails all day and running Susan and Viccy into a tizzy.

CLARA. Did you say that there were two new people?

RUTH. Yes. The other one arrived this afternoon. I gathered from something Susan said that she wasn't really expected.

CLARA. The things you "gather"! How do you do it?

RUTH (*cheerfully*). I'm just the nosey type, dear. Though I expect you would call it "an interest in my fellow humans". (*She puts on a false voice as she says it.*)

CLARA (*giving her a sharp glance*). Mrs. Stacey-Brown. I'm beginning to think I've underestimated you.

RUTH (*yawning*). Oh, no, dear! I'm an open book. Oh! I'm tired.

CLARA. It's no good going to sleep here. You know either Susan or Matron will be in soon. Let's go for a walk.

RUTH. Gosh! You're a glutton for punishment, aren't you?

CLARA. No, but I prefer a walk to a half-hour's session on that foul fixed bicycle.

RUTH (*rising with a groan*). I suppose you're right, but I get so darned hungry when I walk.

CLARA. How many calories are you on now?

RUTH. Just a thousand a day. It's murder!

CLARA (*if she is thin*). I'm up to two thousand five hundred now.

(RUTH *groans*.)

CLARA (*if she is plump*). I've been on a thousand for two weeks and look at me! (*They both groan*.)

RUTH. Dear Heaven! Is it worth it?

CLARA. Don't weaken now—chin up, stiff upper lip and all that nonsense! Think of that "glow of perfect health" and "the peak of physical perfection" that they promised you in the brochure.

RUTH. They forgot to mention all the tortures that we have to go through to get it!

CLARA. Come on. One more torture—a walk.

RUTH. Well, I won't go near the farm. I can't bear the sight of all those pigs—eating!

CLARA (*as they exit*). Very well, we'll go down by the lake, or will the swans upset you?

RUTH (*out of the door*). No. I can take swans, I think.

(*The room is empty for a moment, then* SUSAN LINDY *enters, followed by* RONA WINSTONE. *Susan is in a neat office dress. Rona very smartly but simply dressed. She is obviously nervous, as her hands and quick movements show.*)

SUSAN (*as they enter*). This is my office, although I'm afraid that it is often used as an extra sitting-room. The library is across the hall and the television room upstairs but still guests come here. I suppose that they like to get away from each other at times. (*She is standing at desk, looking at papers.*)

RONA. Yes.

SUSAN. Tea will be served in the common-room in about half an hour.

RONA. I see.

SUSAN. Do sit down, Mrs. Winstone. You look so lost.

RONA (*sitting*). I do feel a little disorientated.

SUSAN. I know. It's like the first day at school. Home is far away, but the gates of prison haven't quite closed round you.

RONA (*mechanically*). Home is far away.

SUSAN. Not that I'm suggesting that this is anything so ghastly as school.

RONA. Didn't you like school?

SUSAN. I loathed it.

RONA. I didn't. It was safe, all your days were planned for you, you just followed. There were no decisions to make. (*She is walking restlessly round the room.*)

SUSAN. I hated being just one of a crowd.

RONA. One can be lost in a crowd.

SUSAN (*looking at her curiously*). That's true. Do sit down, Mrs. Winstone. I want to talk to you about your course.

RONA (*to chair, fireplace*). My what?

SUSAN (*looking at her papers*). I want to find out your wishes about your treatment.

RONA. My treatment? What treatment?

SUSAN. The treatment you came here to obtain.

RONA (*softly*). Canst thou treat a mind diseased?

SUSAN. I beg your pardon.

RONA. I'm sorry. My mind was wandering.

SUSAN. It is usual to plan these things before the guest arrives, but you came so unexpectedly.

RONA. Yes, yes. I didn't know—I didn't know when I could get away.

SUSAN. I see. Well, perhaps you had better wait and see Matron later. Then you can see Victoria about any beauty treatment you require.

RONA (*a little wildly*). Beauty treatment! Yes, perhaps that's what I need. I could go blonde—dye my eyelashes! Hide behind a new face.

SUSAN. Mrs. Winstone—what is it you want?

RONA (*not listening*). But I'd still be here, wouldn't I? It would still be me?

(SUSAN *is looking at her with so puzzled an air that she makes an effort to pull herself together.*)

I'm sorry. I've been under rather a strain lately. (*She takes a cigarette from her bag and lights it.*)

SUSAN. Mrs. Winstone—you did know that this is a health clinic, not an ordinary hotel?

RONA. Yes—yes, of course. (*She pauses.*) No, to tell you the truth, I didn't.

SUSAN. Then why did you come here?

RONA (*hesitates*). For a rest. I remember Jean, my sister-in-law, speaking of this place.

SUSAN. Mrs. Jean Winstone? Yes, she comes here to us for a few weeks every year.

RONA. Does she? That's why it must have stuck in my memory. Jean must have spoken of it several times.

SUSAN (*writing*). I shall put you down for heat, rest and relaxation. Then you can see Viccy. She is our chief beauty counsellor and can advise on any other treatment.

RONA. Thank you. I'll do anything you suggest.

SUSAN (*stands*). I'm sure that after a week of treatment you will feel a great benefit. Now, will you go to the common-room for tea, or would you like it here?

RONA. No, no! Oh! May I have it in my room? I don't want to talk to people just now.

SUSAN. Yes, of course you may, but Matron doesn't encourage meals in your room. She likes to encourage the community spirit.

RONA. I understand, but——

Susan (*kindly*). Try to come down. You will have to meet the other guests eventually.

Rona (*she moves to door*). Yes, yes. I'll try, I'll try to come down. Good-bye. (*She exits.*)

(Susan *looks after her for a second and murmurs to herself "Um—queer", then sits at desk and begins to write. Enter* Victoria Penrose (*known as* Viccy). *She is a slim, very striking girl, beautifully, if a little heavily, made-up. She is the head beauty counsellor in charge of several others whom we do not see, so should look sophisticated, composed and very sure of herself.*)

Viccy (*as she enters*). Hello, Sue! Have you seen that Stacey-Brown woman?

Susan. No. Is she missing again?

Viccy (*sitting on settee arm*). Yes. I don't know why she wastes her money and my time. She's most unco-operative.

Susan. She has oodles of money and I don't think she considers your time very important.

Viccy. But she'll complain at the end of the course if she hasn't got that svelte-like figure that they all want. May the Lord help me!

Susan. I don't think she will. She thinks this whole set-up is a bit of a lark.

Viccy. A lark? For her or for me? Oh! give me a cigarette.

Susan (*handing her a box*). Here you are. Yes, we do find them. Have you seen the new lot?

Viccy. No. What are they like?

Susan (*sitting on left arm settee*). I only got a brief look at Mrs. Heston before she disappeared, but Mrs. Winstone is going to be a real problem.

Viccy (*groaning*). Oh! Not another!

Susan. She's queer. I don't think she came here for treatment at all.

Viccy. Why should anyone pay our prices if she doesn't want treatment?

Susan. I don't know. I think she's running away from something.

Viccy. But why run *here*?

Susan. Yes. Why?

Viccy. Oh, well. I'll deal with her tomorrow. What have you put her down for?

Susan. Relaxation, a little heat therapy and some of your stuff.

Viccy (*indignantly*). My stuff, indeed! I'll have a little more respect from you, my girl, or you'll find me asking for "me cards". (*This is said in a false, common voice.*)

Susan (*with a laugh*). Sorry, Viccy.

(*There is a pause and then* Susan *moves from desk to settee.*)

I wish I could ask for my cards.

Viccy (*lightly*). It's easy. Just say firmly to your aunt—"I want to leave".

Susan. It isn't easy. You know my aunt brought me up ever since my parents died. She paid for my education and did everything for me.

VICCY. And because of that you have to be grateful for the rest of your life?

SUSAN. Well, I do owe her something.

VICCY. Don't you think you've paid it?

SUSAN. What do you mean?

VICCY. How old are you, Sue?

SUSAN. I'm twenty-seven—no, twenty-eight.

VICCY. And you've been working here for the last ten years?

SUSAN. Yes, but——

VICCY. Do you have any salary?

SUSAN. A little, but I'm kept and Aunt often buys me presents of clothes.

VICCY. I think Aunt has a nice bargain.

SUSAN. Perhaps, but I do owe her something.

VICCY. I don't think you owe her a dime! Good grief, girl! Ten years' hard labour! I think that pays a lot.

SUSAN. I should like to get away. Sometimes this place stifles me. But it's impossible.

VICCY. Nonsense! There are heaps of girls who would jump at the chance of a job here. All found in a nice country house, meeting "quate the best pee-o-ple!"

SUSAN. I suppose so.

VICCY. Of course they'd want an adequate salary and they wouldn't expect to be at your aunt's beck and call for twelve hours a day, as you are.

SUSAN. It's no good, Viccy. I can't get away.

VICCY. Never? Are you going to pay for the rest of your life? Don't be a fool!

SUSAN (heatedly and rising). It's easy for you. You are free, I'm not. My aunt depends on me. I can't just walk out on her. You know I can't.

VICCY. On the contrary, darling, I know you can. I know there's a door wide open.

SUSAN (swinging round). You mean—Hugh Barrett?

VICCY. Yes.

SUSAN. How did you know?

VICCY. Heavens alive! Did you really think it was a secret?

SUSAN. But we've been ever so careful.

VICCY. Oh! Very careful, but it is extraordinary the number of times our handsome veterinary surgeon has had to be called in lately.

SUSAN. Oh!

VICCY. And the number of times when he has "happened to be in the district" and has called in. (She laughs.)

SUSAN (weakly). We have had a lot of trouble lately with one of the horses.

VICCY. How kind of him.

SUSAN. Tell me, do you think my aunt knows?

VICCY (shrugs). Perhaps! She's pretty cute; she doesn't miss much.

SUSAN. I wish I knew what to do.

VICCY. I don't want to be indelicate, darling, but has he declared himself?

SUSAN (*with a short laugh*). Yes. He wants us to get married quite soon.

VICCY. That's splendid. I couldn't be more pleased. Do it before the end of the summer and then I can be a bridesmaid.

SUSAN. I've told him I can't.

VICCY. What! You want your head examined! Me, I'd grab him with two hands. He's bliss, my dear, pure bliss.

SUSAN. I can't marry and leave my aunt—not yet, anyway. I must get her used to the idea and then find her another secretary.

VICCY. Get her used to the idea? What do you mean? Surely she must have expected that you'd marry one day?

SUSAN. No. I'm sure she's never thought of it. She always speaks as if I'm here for ever. She's promised me a partnership when I'm older.

VICCY. She what? (*Amazed.*)

SUSAN. Promised me a partnership.

VICCY. Well! Blow me down! There's a double-crossing old so-and-so for you!

SUSAN. What do you mean?

VICCY. Because three months ago she promised *me* that. I'd threatened to leave. You remember? I told you at the time.

SUSAN. Yes. I do remember you said something about leaving. Then my aunt told me that she'd persuaded you to reconsider the idea.

VICCY. She *did*—under a promise of a part share in the business. There! Can't you see how much her promises are worth? I'd thank her for nothing. You want your own life, not hers, not even for the promise of "pie in the sky".

SUSAN. She doesn't see it like that.

VICCY. Now, look here, Sue, you've got to take this chance. You'd be a fool if you let it go, just because your aunt won't like losing you.

SUSAN. But I do——

VICCY. Listen! She's been good to you, yes. But you've repaid her for that many times over. You mustn't let her spoil your life. You grab Hugh before someone else comes along and does so.

SUSAN. I wish I knew what to do. I don't want to hurt her.

VICCY. You must tell her tonight and then set about finding that secretary.

SUSAN (*miserably*). I'll try.

VICCY. Get out, Sue. I give you my blessing. I'll even stage-manage the elopement if it comes to that! (*She laughs.*)

SUSAN. Oh, Viccy!

VICCY (*at the door*). I must go and see my relaxation class. I left old Lady Coulsden under gentle heat. She'll be fried a nice brown now. See you later, and think about my advice.

SUSAN. Thanks, Viccy. I will.

(VICCY *exits and* SUSAN *returns to desk, where she sits and stares ahead, deep in thought. After a moment the door opens and* ERICA HESTON *stands in the entrance.*)

(*Turning and rising.*) Oh! Mrs. Heston. I didn't see you.

MRS. H. May I come in?

SUSAN. Yes, do. This is supposed to be my office but when we have a large number of guests it gets used as an extra sitting-room.

MRS. H. I see.

SUSAN. Tea should be served by now. Would you like me to have a tray sent in for you?

MRS. H. (*on settee*). Not at the moment. I'd like to talk to you. Come and sit down.

(SUSAN *moves to chair near fireplace*.)

SUSAN. Have you seen Matron about your treatment?

MRS. H. Not yet. I'll see her later.

SUSAN. I don't believe you've been here before, have you, Mrs. Heston?

MRS. H. No. I've only just found out—er—heard about this place.

SUSAN. We never advertise, we have no need to, we keep so very busy.

MRS. H. You must have a very good reputation.

SUSAN. Yes. My aunt—er—Matron is very proud of her reputation.

MRS. H. Is she indeed?

SUSAN. This place is her life. It is really all she cares about.

MRS. H. Yes. I can understand that. It must be very profitable.

SUSAN. I suppose it is, but we give very good value. Our treatments are given by experts. We have a resident doctor, *and* all the amenities of a first-class hotel.

MRS. H. Oh, yes. I can see you give all the trimmings.

SUSAN (*indignant*). Trimmings!

MRS. H. (*with a laugh*). Take no notice of me, I'm a cynic. I once worked in one of these places. That would turn anyone into a cynic. Dealing with fat, selfish, self-centred women for months at a time.

SUSAN. I don't see it like that at all. People come to us with a problem and we help them to solve it.

MRS. H. Don't tell me you are still starry-eyed? You know, you aren't quite the type for this set-up.

SUSAN. What do you mean?

MRS. H. Oh! This kind of place is usually run by a few of the sergeant-major type and a couple of dim, dedicated spinsters.

SUSAN. Oh!

MRS. H. Why do you stay here? Is the pay all that good?

SUSAN. It has nothing to do with the pay.

MRS. H. Then why? You must get sick as hell of it at times.

SUSAN. I do—but—I'm sorry, Mrs. Heston. I shouldn't be talking to you like this. You can have no possible interest in my difficulties.

MRS. H. On the contrary, I've been most interested.

SUSAN (*standing*). Would you like me to ask Milly to bring the tea here?

MRS. H. Thanks. That would be a great relief.

SUSAN. Relief from what?

MRS. H. The gentle sparring in the lounge. "*Do* have that chocolate cake, Mrs. Brown. It's the last one." Or, "Will you have another sandwich, dear Mrs. Jones?" (*She laughs.*)

SUSAN (*laughing*). Really, Mrs. Heston! It isn't like that.

Mrs. H. Oh, yes it is, only worse, much worse.

Susan. Well, we don't have chocolate cake. You are lucky if you get half an "Energen" biscuit.

Mrs. H. (*with a groan*). Oh, yes! I'd forgotten that. Well, I suppose I can stick it for a while.

Susan. Why did you come here, if it wasn't for treatment?

Mrs. H. Various reasons.

Susan. I see. Now you haven't seen Matron yet. Shall I fix up your interview for later this evening?

Mrs. H. Yes. You do that.

Susan (*looking a little surprised at her tone*). Very well. Now, I'll get Milly to bring in some tea. I'll see you later. (*She exits.*)

(Mrs. Heston *moves to chair by fireplace, opens her bag and lights a cigarette. She moves the chair slightly so that her back is to the door and she is not easily seen. After a pause the door opens and* Rona Winstone *enters.* Rona *does not see* Mrs. H. *She moves to the desk, hesitates, puts her hand on the telephone, hesitates again, sits in chair and looks at telephone. Then, obviously making up her mind, she picks up the receiver.*)

Rona. Will you get me Carnstone 4415? Yes, double four, one five. Yes. I'll wait. (*She drums her fingers on the desk as she waits.*) Hello! Oh! Who is that? Oh, it's you, Helen. Is Mr. Winstone in? . . . Not at all? . . . I see. Very well. No, there's no message. Now I'll speak to Nannie. Yes, Helen, I'm sure you will . . . just fetch Nannie, will you? (*There is a long pause.*) Oh! Hello, Nannie! How are the children? . . . Good . . . Good . . . No cough at all now? Splendid! . . . Did she really? . . . How funny! (*Her face is alight.*) Oh! The pet. No, no, Nannie. I cannot get back for a day or so. (*Her face is set.*) Yes. I'll let you know. Take care of them for me. . . . Yes, I know you will. . . . Good-bye . . . Yes, I'll ring again tomorrow. . . . Good-bye, Nannie.

(Rona *puts down the receiver and her control goes; her head on her hands, she cries bitterly.* Mrs. Heston *leaves her for a moment, and then speaks.*)

Mrs. H. Nothing can be quite as bad as that.

(Rona *gives one startled look at her and goes on crying.* Mrs. H. *rises and goes to her.*)

What is the matter? Oh, *don't* cry like that. Nothing is ever as bad as it seems. Take my word for that!

(Rona *struggles to obtain control of herself.*)

Here, come over here and sit down. (*She moves* Rona *to settee, sits beside her and offers her a cigarette.*) Cigarette?

(Rona *takes cigarette with trembling hands, and* Mrs. H. *lights it for her.*)

That's better. No, don't speak. Wait until you feel better. I'm sorry I overheard that conversation, but you were speaking before I knew that you were in the room.

Rona. It doesn't matter.

Mrs. H. Now, I don't know what is wrong but I do know that nothing is as bad as it seems. Everything passes. Remember that—everything passes.

RONA. Everything passes? Does it? Everything?

MRS. H. Yes. Just give it time. Ha! Here comes tea. That will do you good.

(*Enter* MILLY TIPTON. *She is a middle-aged woman, dressed in a neat blue overall. She carries a tea-tray which she sets on the low table near the settee.*)

MILLY (*as she enters*). Miss Susan asked me to bring this. I put on some extra cups in case anyone else comes in. (*She bends over the tray, arranging the things, her back to* MRS. HESTON.) Never know where to serve tea, I don't. Sometimes it's one room and sometimes another. Thought *this* room was meant to be Miss Susan's office, *not* another sitting-room.

MRS. H. (*clearly*). Thank you, Milly.

(MILLY *swings round and starts back, looking at* MRS. HESTON *in amazement.*)

MILLY. Oh! My Gawd! How did *you* get here?

MRS. H. In the usual way, Milly.

MILLY. What you doing here? Why you come?

MRS. H. Why, Milly, you don't seem very pleased to see me?

MILLY. I'm not!

MRS. H. Such an old friend, too. How many years is it? Twenty-seven? Twenty-eight?

MILLY. Thought you was dead by now.

MRS. H. Wishful thinking, Milly! I'm alive—and kicking.

MILLY. Well! You better go and do your kicking somewhere else. We don't want you here.

MRS. H. How unkind of you, Milly! After all these years of friendship.

MILLY. You was never our friend.

MRS. H. Oh, yes. I was. I was a very good friend—once.

MILLY. That was a long time ago. What you come back for now?

MRS. H. Just to visit old friends.

MILLY. Like heck you have! You are up to no good!

MRS. H. Oh, Milly! How you misjudge me.

MILLY. Does Matron know you are here?

MRS. H. Not yet. I suppose she knows *a* Mrs. Heston is here, but I don't think she realizes——

MILLY. That it's *you*?

MRS. H. No—and I don't want you to tell her. Do you understand *that*, Milly? You are *not* to tell her. I promise you it will be unpleasant for you if you do.

MILLY. Oh! I won't tell her. None of *my* business—any of it.

MRS. H. (*softly*). That's right, Milly. It's none of your business. Let's keep it that way, shall we?

MILLY (*as she exits*). Coming back here—bet you cause trouble. You always have. (*Grumbling, she exits.*)

MRS. H. (*blandly, as she turns to* RONA). Forgive that little episode. As you will have gathered, I knew Milly some years ago.

RONA (*politely*). Yes.

MRS. H. She was always a rather difficult character, one of these old retainers. Trying, but a treasure. I'm sure you understand.

RONA (*not understanding*). Yes, of course. We have several of them in our own family.

MRS. H. (*moving to settee*). Now for some tea. Sugar and milk?

RONA. A little of both, please.

(MRS. H. *pours tea for them both. Enter* LADY COULSDEN. *She is a rather tottery old lady of over seventy. Her voice is wavering, but still slightly imperious. She walks with a stick and carries a knitting-bag.*)

LADY C. Ah! May I join you? So many people in the other room, they confuse me.

MRS. H. Of course. Where would you like to sit?

LADY C. (*to chair downstage*). This will do for me. (*Sits.*) I don't think I know you?

MRS. H. My name is Mrs. Heston, and this is?——

RONA. Rona Winstone.

LADY C. I am Lady Harvey Coulsden. I expect you know the name. My husband was Governor of Balistan for many years.

MRS. H. How interesting for you.

LADY C. (*babbling on*). Oh, yes, it was! A most interesting time. It had, of course, its responsibilities, but one cannot have power without responsibility, can one? Ah! We spent many happy years out there. It is sad to think that I am alone now.

MRS. H. You have no family?

LADY C. No. I never had any children. My responsibilities as a hostess left me no time to have a family. It didn't seem to matter then, but since—— (*She sighs.*)

MRS. H. Have you no relatives?

LADY C. Oh, yes. I have a nephew and a niece. I live with them now. They are very good—very good, but old people become very tiresome; yes, that must be it, very tiresome.

RONA. Can I give you some tea?

LADY C. What did you say? Tea? Yes, thank you.

(RONA *pours tea and* MRS. H. *takes it to* LADY C.)

How are you getting on here? Do you know that I can run up fifteen stairs now?

MRS. H. Can you indeed? (*Takes tea from* RONA *and sits chair up fireplace.*)

LADY C. Can you run up fifteen stairs?

MRS. H. I've no intention of trying.

LADY C. Yes, fifteen! Isn't that good? And Viccy says my reflexes are wonderful for my age. How are your reflexes?

MRS. H. Ghastly, I should think——if I have any.

LADY C. (*sipping her tea*). Yes. Viccy is very pleased with me. Fifteen stairs is very good, isn't it? Of course I do get a little tired, but one mustn't give up. Viccy says that self-discipline is all-important. Do you practise self-discipline?

MRS. H. Never.

LADY C. Oh! I try to. I try every day— Viccy says— Oh! I've forgotten what Viccy says—— (*She looks distressed.*)

RONA (*kindly*). I shouldn't worry. You'll remember later. Just drink your tea and relax.

LADY C. But I ought to remember.

RONA. Don't worry.

(LADY C. *puts down her cup and leans back in chair.*)

LADY C. I should be knitting. I've started a jersey for Miriam's youngest and I must get it finished. The last time I started a jersey he grew out of it before I had finished it. So confusing—— (*Her head is nodding.*)

MRS. H. There will be plenty of time tomorrow.

LADY C. (*drowsily*). Plenty of time— Self-dis-ci-pline—— (*She sleeps.*)

MRS. H. (*after a pause*). Self-discipline at her age! It's positively criminal!

RONA. Poor dear!

MRS. H. I don't suppose there's a soul in the world that really cares about her. The tragedy of lonely old age.

RONA. It's queer, isn't it—that when you are young you never contemplate old age, yet it is *then* that you are shaping its pattern.

MRS. H. (*she lights cigarette, offers case to* RONA, *who shakes her head*). How very profound of you! (*Cynically.*)

(*Enter* RUTH STACEY-BROWN *and* CLARA FANTON.)

RUTH. Hello! The two new girls both hiding in Susan's room. You found this hidey-hole pretty quickly!

CLARA. Mrs. Ransome in the common-room is discovering for the sixtieth time that she has lost ten pounds. So we faded quickly.

RONA. Can I pour you some tea?

RUTH. Thanks—no milk—but just *show* it the sugar, will you?

CLARA. Thank you. No sugar.

(RONA *pours tea and it is handed round.* CLARA *sits on the settee,* RUTH *pulls out chair from behind desk.*)

RUTH. I heard that you'd both arrived. Er—my name is Stacey-Brown. I come here every year.

CLARA. To the dismay of Viccy! I'm Clara Fanton.

MRS. H. My name is Heston—Erica Heston.

RONA. And I'm Rona Winstone.

RUTH. How are you settling? Have you seen our glamorous Viccy yet?

MRS. H. No. That is a pleasure so far deferred.

RONA. She sounds rather intimidating.

CLARA. She's a horror, but she gets results.

MRS. H. Results?

RUTH. The body beautiful!

CLARA. That peak of physical fitness!

RUTH. That streamlined figure!

MRS. H. All that?

RONA. How terrible!

RUTH. Terrible! That's what you are paying for.

RONA. Am I?

CLARA. You are! Wait till you see the bill. That usually frightens you so much you lose ten pounds at once.

RUTH. Are there any biscuits?

RONA. Yes. Here they are. (*Holding out plate.*)

RUTH (*taking one*). Thanks.

CLARA. That's fifteen calories!

RUTH (*hesitating*). Oh! Curse it! I can't help it. After that walk I am starving.

CLARA (*chanting*). One second in the mouth—two ounces on the hips!

RUTH. Stop it, you wretch! I get enough of that from Viccy.

CLARA (*to* MRS. H.). Have you had your skin test yet?

MRS. H. No. What is that?

CLARA. Oh, a microscopic examination to discover if your skin is suffering from lack of nourishment, over-oiliness, over-dryness, etc., etc. (*She chants.*)

MRS. H. How disgusting!

CLARA. Mine looked like the mountains of the moon.

MRS. H. Have they discovered the cure?

CLARA. Oh, yes. I've just got the craters of the moon now. (*They laugh.*)

RONA. Surely one isn't forced to undergo all these tortures?

RUTH. Not exactly forced, dear, but wait until you've seen Matron. She'll convince you that your future happiness depends on deep therapy, strenuous exercise, Viccy's ministrations and complete starvation. She'll have you *begging* for it! You'll see.

MRS. H. I can't wait to meet her.

RONA. But they all sound so horrifying.

RUTH. They are!

CLARA. If she really forces too much on you, then you can see Susan. She can usually arrange a modified programme.

MRS. H. Ah! Susan! She seems a nice girl.

RUTH. She's a poppet! How she stands that aunt of hers I don't know.

CLARA. I should have run—years ago.

MRS. H. Surely she could go if she wished.

CLARA. No. I don't think it's so easy as that.

RUTH. Auntie has no intention of losing the perfect, cut-price secretary.

MRS. H. I see.

RONA. Poor Susan! She seems such a nice girl.

CLARA. She is. She's the only completely human person in this place.

RUTH (*taking another biscuit*). Here's another two ounces.

CLARA. If Viccy could see you!

RUTH. There would be a distinctly unpleasant interview with Matron. "Mrs. Stacey-Brown, we cannot help you if you lack the self-discipline to help yourself." (*Said in a false high-toned voice. She stops aghast as the*

B

door opens and the MATRON *stands just inside. She is an erect, stern-looking woman, dressed in black. She looks at* RUTH *and* CLARA *but does not see* MRS. H., *who is in the high-backed chair, facing fireplace.*)

MATRON. Mrs. Stacey-Brown. Victoria reports that you have not completed your exercises today.

RUTH. I—er—went for a walk instead.

MATRON. Then you should have informed Victoria of that fact. (*Turns to* CLARA.) I believe that you are required in the massage room, Miss Fanton.

CLARA. Yes, Matron (*looking at watch*). I shall be there in a few minutes.

MATRON. With so many guests requiring treatments we must keep to a strict time schedule. You understand?

CLARA. Yes, Matron.

MATRON (*moving into room*). Ah! Mrs. Winstone, we must—— (*Her voice dies away as she sees* MRS. HESTON. *Her hand clutches the back of the settee.* MRS. H. *slowly stands.*) You, oh! You! (*She is speechless.*)

MRS. H. Yes, Emilia Dale, it is I.

(MATRON *tries to speak but cannot. They all hold the tableau as curtain descends.*)

CURTAIN.

ACT II.

SCENE 1.

SCENE *is the same, two days later. It is early evening and the lamp on the desk is alight, and the curtains pulled over the window.* LADY COULSDEN *is in the chair downstage fireplace. She holds her knitting but is leaning back with her eyes closed.* MRS. STACEY-BROWN *is on the settee, a book in her hand. She is obviously chewing a sweet and, during the early part of the scene, she secretly slips a sweet from her bag to her mouth.* RONA WINSTONE *is in the chair above fireplace. She is smoking, her hands twisting the cigarette nervously. They all wear simple semi-evening dresses.*

RUTH. I am sure it was what is called "a pregnant moment"—but what is "pregged" I have no idea. Have you?

RONA. No.

RUTH. Matron has been out of circulation. I gather that she's been giving Susan, Viccy and the others absolute hell.

RONA. Has she?

RUTH. Yes, and Mrs. Heston told me, in the nicest possible way, to mind my own business when I asked her what it was all about. (*She laughs.*) Isn't it infuriating?

RONA. I don't think it wise to inquire too deeply into other people's lives. We all have our secret places.

RUTH. I'll say! And this is yours, isn't it?

RONA (*startled*). What do you mean?

RUTH. You didn't come here for treatment, did you? You didn't even know this was a clinic. You came here to escape?

RONA. I—I—— (*She is at a loss for words.*)

RUTH. I wonder what you are escaping from?

LADY C. (*suddenly*). Mrs. Stacey-Brown, you are being rude and impertinent.

(RONA *and* RUTH *look surprised.*)

As I get older I realize more and more that each of us hides something and that we are all entitled to keep that away from prying eyes.

RUTH. I didn't——

LADY C. So, Mrs. Stacey-Brown, in the nicest possible way, I say, Shut up! (*She sinks back into her chair and closes her eyes.*)

RUTH. Hey! I've been bitten by a mouse! Sorry, Mrs. Winstone, I didn't mean to pry. I guess I'm just nosey and I speak first and think afterwards.

RONA. It's all right. I—I am—escaping, but I can't speak about it yet.

RUTH. That's all right, dear. You slap me down if I ask too many questions. I need it at times.

RONA (*with a smile*). I will.

LADY C. I remember when we were in the Service there was a general's wife. What was her name?— Never mind. She was a charming woman, quite charming, yes, really very popular, but so—so inquisitive. In the end I had to withhold my invitations to Government House. I was sorry to take such a drastic step, but I had to do it—— (*Her voice fades away.* RUTH *and* RONA *have been listening with obvious patience.*)

RUTH (*cheerfully*). I guess that taught her a lesson.

LADY C. Yes, yes. I remember once when we were in Siam—er—was it Siam? No, perhaps it was in— Oh, I forget— Yes, I remember—what was it I was going to tell you?

RONA (*kindly*). I shouldn't bother. How did your treatment go today?

LADY C. Oh, very well, though I think Viccy forgets me at times. I'm sure I was far too long under heat therapy.

RONA. But that is very soothing.

LADY C. Yes, yes. Do you know that I can run up fifteen stairs? Isn't that wonderful?

(RUTH *makes a grimace.*)

RONA. Yes, wonderful.

(*Enter* CLARA FANTON, *followed by* TESSA DARKE. *Tessa is an actress who is resting between shows. She is in an ultra-smart cocktail dress and is very well made-up. She speaks in a high, brittle tone and rather obviously drapes herself against furniture.*)

CLARA (*as they enter*). Hello! May I introduce a new girl. This is Mrs. Darke. Mrs. Darke, this is Mrs. Stacey-Brown, Mrs. Winstone, and Lady Coulsden.

(*They all nod and murmur their greetings in various ways.*)

RUTH (*indicating settee*). Come and sit here, Mrs. Darke.

TESSA. Oh! Don't call me Mrs. Darke. It makes me feel so aged. Call me Tessa. (*She sits.*)

CLARA (*sitting chair near desk*). Tessa arrived this afternoon. I've just rescued her from Mrs. Ransome.

TESSA. Who, I gather, had lost ten pounds!

RONA. Have you been here before, Mrs. Darke—er—Tessa?

TESSA. Yes. I try to come at least once a year.

RUTH. Me too, but is it worth it?

TESSA. I think so. In my profession it's vital I keep slim.

RUTH. Your——?

TESSA. I'm an actress.

(LADY COULSDEN *shoots a suspicious glance at her.*)

RUTH. Ah! You have a real reason for being here.

TESSA. Haven't you?

CLARA. Ruth comes because she goes to the south of France every summer and wants to display a swim suit.

RUTH. Yes, and I haven't character enough to diet unless I'm made to do so.

CLARA. And not even then!

(RUTH *makes a grimace at* CLARA.)

LADY C. I can run up fifteen stairs now.

Tessa (*coldly*). How nice for you. (*To the others.*) What about a drink before dinner?

Clara ⎱ (*together*). A drink!
Ruth ⎰

Tessa (*ringing bell near fireplace*). Yes. I guess I need it.

Clara. You'll never get one.

Ruth. All those calories.

Tessa. I'll get one.

Clara. If Matron finds out——

Tessa. I've dealt with Matron before.

Ruth. Then you are a better man than I am!

(*Enter* Milly.)

Tessa. Would you mind bringing some sherry and glasses, Milly?

Milly. Sherry?

Tessa. Sherry—that brown stuff in a bottle.

Milly. I don't think it's allowed.

Tessa. It is if I order it, Milly. Go on. I'll deal with Matron.

Milly. Very well, Miss, if that's an order.

Tessa. It is, Milly, it is.

Milly (*as she goes*). Well, I don't know—sherry!

Clara. That I should live to see such bravery! (*They all laugh.*)

Tessa. One must be civilized.

Lady C. When we were in India we had a drink at six o'clock every evening—at six o'clock precisely. I must admit I do miss it a little. (*She nods her head.*)

Ruth (*to* Tessa). You, I can see, will be an asset to this community. How long are you staying?

Tessa. Just two weeks. Then I fly to Australia to rehearse for a new play.

Clara. It's a shame that "The Golden Days" folded up so quickly. I thought that you were very good in it.

(*At these words* Rona *reacts violently, unnoticed by the others.*)

Tessa. It lasted six months. That's not bad these days.

Ruth. "The Golden Days"—were you in that?

Tessa. Yes. I played Fenella.

(Rona *stands up and moves blindly towards the door.*)

Ruth. Of course. How silly of me not to recognize you. You are Tessa Trevallion. (*Then, noticing* Rona.) What's the matter with Mrs. Winstone?

Rona. I—er—forgive me—I— (*She runs from the room.* Ruth *and* Clara *look at each other.*)

Clara. What's wrong with her?

Ruth. I don't know.

Tessa. Did you say Winstone? Is she Mrs. Winstone—er—Mrs. Ralph Winstone?

Clara. Yes. Do you know her?

Tessa. No.

RUTH. But something you said upset her.

TESSA. Did it?

CLARA. She's been acting rather queerly ever since she came here.

RUTH. She seemed all right before you two came in. I tried to find out what was wrong.

CLARA. You would.

RUTH. I just got slapped down. Lady Coulsden was quite unkind to me.

(*She looks at* LADY C. *and laughs.*)

LADY C. (*rising*). I merely rebuked your inquisitiveness. I think I shall rest for awhile before dinner. I find all this chat quite tiring. (*She exits.*)

TESSA. We can consider ourselves dismissed.

RUTH. Never an invitation to Government House. (*They laugh.*)

CLARA. Poor old soul! Let her keep her dignity. It's all she has left.

(*Enter* MILLY, *carrying tray of sherry and glasses.*)

MILLY. Here you are! I saw Miss Victoria and she says Mrs. Stacey-Brown should not indulge and she advises only one glass each for you others.

TESSA. Thank you, Milly. My compliments to Viccy and tell her——

CLARA (*quickly*). We shall be quite moderate, Milly, quite moderate.

MILLY (*as she goes*). So I should hope. (*She exits.*)

CLARA. Haven't you yet learned that it can be very unpleasant here if you annoy Viccy?

TESSA (*moving to desk and pouring sherry*). I couldn't care less about Viccy. I know that I can shed about a stone in a couple of weeks here. That's all I ask. (*She hands sherry to the others.*)

CLARA (*as she sips her sherry*). Ah! Nice, very nice.

RUTH. Isn't it infuriating that all the nicest things in life are either immoral or fattening! (*They laugh.*)

CLARA. As I reach middle age I begin to wonder whether either of those things are worth evading. (*She laughs to show she is not serious.*)

TESSA. Only the latter, darling, only the latter.

RUTH (*as she finishes her sherry*). That was very nice.

TESSA. Have another?

RUTH. Thank you. Who was it said: "I can resist anything but temptation"? (*She hands her glass to* TESSA, *who refills it.*)

TESSA (*to* CLARA). More for you?

CLARA. No thanks. It will take half an hour on that loathsome bike to get this off. (*She rises.*) I must go and see Viccy. I want to change my massage period tomorrow. I missed her after tea. Thanks for the sherry, Tessa.

TESSA. Oh! Glad you could join me.

(CLARA *exits. There is the sound of a gong.*)

RUTH (*as she sips*). Ah! There's dinner. For once I do not join in the stampede.

TESSA. I shall in a few days time. Imagine running for carrot soup! (*They laugh.*) Tell me, when did Mrs. Winstone come here?

RUTH. Two days ago, I think.

Tessa. Ah!

Ruth. What does that cryptic sound mean? You said you didn't know Mrs. Winstone.

Tessa. I don't, but I know her husband.

Ruth (*in imitation*). Ah!

Tessa. Ah! indeed. (*The gong rings again.*)

Ruth. Now I understand——

(*Enter* Matron.)

Matron. Ladies, the gong has rung twice.

Tessa (*stands and puts down glass*). For whom the bell tolls!

Ruth. We were just going, Matron.

Matron. You understand we cannot delay dinner, owing to staff difficulties.

Tessa. We go—we go.

Ruth. Of course, Matron.

Matron. I should like to see you later, Mrs. Darke, to arrange your schedule.

Tessa. Very well, Matron.

(*Exit* Tessa *and* Ruth.)

(Matron *picks up glasses and puts them on tray, with a look of distaste on her face. Then she rings bell and returns to desk, picking up some papers. Enter* Milly.)

Matron. Remove this, please (*indicating tray*). Who gave permission for sherry to be served?

Milly. Miss Victoria. Mrs. Darke ordered it and, as it was her first evening, Miss Victoria said she could have it.

Matron. I see. Please ask *my* permission in future, will you, Milly?

Milly. Yes, Matron.

Matron. Now ask Miss Susan to come here, will you?

Milly. Yes, Matron. (*She exits.*)

(*There is a short pause and then* Susan *enters. She is dressed in a coat, with a scarf over her head.*)

Susan. Did you want me, Aunt? I was just going out.

Matron. Out? At this hour?

Susan. I've been so busy, I haven't been outside all day.

Matron. But you'll miss dinner.

Susan. It doesn't matter. Milly will make me a sandwich later.

Matron. I don't like you missing your meals, Susan.

Susan. Aunt! Isn't that rather funny from you, who spends her days telling everyone that they eat too much?

Matron. The women who come here spend the whole year eating. You don't—and you work very hard.

Susan. That is why I want to go out. I must get away from this place sometimes.

Matron. Of course, but not now. Take some time off tomorrow. Go into Shelford. There are several things I need from there.

SUSAN. Of course I'll go to Shelford for you if you want me to, but now I wish to go for a walk.

MATRON. Susan!

SUSAN. Yes. (*Turning back.*)

MATRON. You are meeting someone?

SUSAN. Yes.

MATRON. Who?

SUSAN (*pulls off scarf*). I think you know or you wouldn't be questioning me like this.

MATRON. Yes. I do know. It's that man—Hugh Barrett—isn't it?

SUSAN. Yes.

MATRON. Do you think it is wise?

SUSAN. Wise? What do you mean?

MATRON. Is it wise to meet this man, about whom you know so little?

SUSAN. Oh! Aunt! Don't keep calling him "this man". You've known Hugh for the past two years.

MATRON. I know him as a veterinary surgeon, but that's all.

SUSAN. How could you know any more of him when you've persistently snubbed any friendly move he has made towards us?

MATRON. I saw no reason for any but a purely business relationship.

SUSAN. There you are! Whenever I make any friends outside this place you freeze them off.

MATRON. Nonsense!

SUSAN (*heatedly*). It isn't nonsense. I never meet anyone but the guests here. Even on holiday you isolate us, so that no one gets beyond the "Good-morning! Isn't it fine?" stage.

MATRON. That isn't true! We've met some very nice people on holiday.

SUSAN. Oh, yes! All over fifty. Anyone under that age is suspect immediately.

MATRON. Why are you talking like this? Haven't I always considered *you*—ever since your parents died——

SUSAN (*with a sigh*). Yes. I know. You've been very good to me and I'm very grateful but——   ,

MATRON. But you still insist on going to meet this—er—Mr. Barrett?

SUSAN. Yes— Oh! Aunt, why must you make an issue of this now?

MATRON. Because I know you are making a mistake. What can this young man offer you? He lives in that miserable little cottage near the river and I should think his practice is quite small.

SUSAN. It is, but it's growing.

MATRON. It's chicken-feed against this place, Susan. You do the books. You know how much we make each year.

SUSAN. Yes. I know.

MATRON. It will be yours one day—all yours.

SUSAN. Suppose I say I don't want it?

MATRON. You couldn't be such a fool. I've spent my life building up this business—all for you.

SUSAN. All for me? Has it been all for me?

MATRON. Of course it has. You are all I've got, Susan. You can't let me down now—not now, just as the place is becoming really profitable.

Susan. But Aunt——

Matron. Listen, Sue. Forget this man, give me another year—or two years. Then we'll sell this place and you can do as you like—travel—anything. Just another year, that's all I ask.

Susan. I don't know what to say.

Matron. I can't do without you, Susan. You know how much I depend on you, and you do owe me something for all the years I've looked after you.

Susan (*miserably*). I know.

Matron. Heavens! You are only young yet. There will be other, better men. Don't throw everything away because of a fleeting emotional entanglement.

Susan. But I——

Matron. Just one year, Susan. Can't you give me that?

Susan. I—I'll try, Aunt. But I must see Hugh now. I must talk to him.

Matron. Write him a note.

Susan. No. I must see him.

Matron. Don't be foolish. Do as I say and——

Susan (*almost in tears*). Oh! Leave me alone, Aunt. I suppose I'll have to stay with you, but let me do things my own way.

(Susan *runs from the room.* Matron *looks after her, makes a step towards the door, and then, with a sigh of satisfaction, moves back to desk. There is a pause, and then* Mrs. Heston *walks in.*)

Mrs. H. That, Emilia Dale, was most edifying.

Matron (*swinging round*). You! You were listening!

Mrs. H. Certainly I was. It's one of my nicer traits—listening at doors.

Matron. And much good may it do you!

Mrs. H. Oh! But it has, several times. Once, you remember, I did more—I peeped!

Matron. Be quiet! Why did you come here?

Mrs. H. Just to see how my old friend and her——

Matron. Will you keep quiet! You have no business here. We parted years ago. Why have you come back now?

Mrs. H. Now, *that* is the sixty-four-dollar question. Shall we say I have two reasons.

Matron. And what are they?

Mrs. H. I am very interested in dear Susan.

Matron. Nonsense! You only knew her for a few months.

Mrs. H. Ah, yes! Those few months in Italy, hidden away in a little lost village. How lovely it was!

Matron. It rained for most of the time, the villa was unheated, and you loathed every minute of it.

Mrs. H. As you did, my dear Emilia.

Matron. Yes, as I did.

Mrs. H. Still, I've often wondered what became of Susan.

Matron. What do you think could become of her? She's grown up in the usual way.

MRS. H. Yes. A pretty girl, too. Pity she hasn't married.

MATRON. Susan is quite happy as she is.

MRS. H. That's what you think!

MATRON. Susan's life is nothing to do with you. Will you mind your own business?

MRS. H. Hasn't it? Remember, I dandled her on my knee once.

MATRON. Stop trying to be sentimental. It doesn't suit you. Tell me, why have you come here?

MRS. H. To see you.

MATRON. Why?

MRS. H. Shall we say for old times' sake?

MATRON. No! We will not. You never liked me, Erica Heston. You helped me once. I admit that, but you were well paid for it.

MRS. H. Was I? What a pity it was such a long time ago! One's memory fades so much—for some things.

MATRON. Will you say what you want, and then get out of here?

MRS. H. (*softly*). Just this place, Emilia, that is all.

MATRON (*stunned*). What did you say?

MRS. H. I want this place—or part of it. Is that plain enough?

MATRON. Over my dead body!

MRS. H. Or over mine?— Is that what you are thinking?

MATRON. I owe you nothing. Any debt to you was paid, and amply paid, years ago.

MRS. H. Oh, yes! I was paid for services rendered. Now I want paying for something else.

MATRON. For what?

MRS. H. For keeping my mouth shut.

MATRON. Blackmail!

MRS. H. Hush your mouth! Don't say such nasty words.

MATRON (*going to her*). Get out of here! Go on, get out! I won't have you in my house.

MRS. H. Now! Now! Take it easy! I came here as a legitimate guest. I have letters arranging my treatment for two weeks. That's a contract. You can't throw me out.

MATRON. I can. You are unsuitable for treatment. You don't respond.

MRS. H. I haven't had any treatment yet, and when I do I'll respond all right. Oh! How I'll respond! (*She laughs.*)

MATRON (*trying to pull herself together*). Look! If you need it I'll give you some money—hundred pounds. Take that and go.

MRS. H. A hundred pounds! Really, my dear Emilia, you are quite amusing. Do you think I don't know how much you are raking in over this little racket?

MATRON. How dare you!

MRS. H. (*continuing*). I've worked in several of these places. I'm a trained physiotherapist. You didn't know that, did you? Yes. I used that little—er—gift you gave me so many years ago to get some training.

MATRON. Then you don't need——

MRS. H. (*holding up her hand*). Listen to me! I'm not a big, bad wolf, here to rob you of your hard-earned wages. I can help you——

(MATRON *snorts*.)

Oh, yes. I can. I'd be good in a place like this. But I don't just want a job. I'm tired of slaving for £10 a week. I want a part share.

MATRON. Never! I won't——

MRS. H. Now, don't make up your mind too quickly. I'd be very useful to you, but don't forget I can be very—er—shall we say upsetting? Just you think it over, Emilia, just think it over.

(*She laughs and walks from the room.* MATRON *sinks on settee with her head in her hands, and then* VICCY *enters*.)

VICCY (*as she enters carrying papers*). Ah! There you are, Matron! Can I see you about— Are you ill?

MATRON. No—no. I have a headache, that is all. What is it you wanted?

VICCY. Just these time schedules.

MATRON. Leave them until tomorrow.

VICCY. But I——

MATRON. Tomorrow, I said.

VICCY (*turning to go*). Very well.

MATRON (*calling her back*). Viccy?

VICCY. Yes, Matron.

MATRON. This Mrs. Heston who has just arrived——

VICCY. Yes, Matron.

MATRON. Were her treatments arranged before she came?

VICCY. Yes, Matron.

MATRON. What were they? Can you remember?

VICCY. Yes. The modified diet, hip vibration, toning massage and—that's all, I think.

MATRON. No electrical treatment?

VICCY. No. I don't think so.

MATRON. Have you treated her yet?

VICCY. I supervised the hip vibration yesterday. That's all.

MATRON. Has she talked to Susan?

VICCY (*surprised*). A little, I think. I don't know.

MATRON (*turning away*). She's—she's a woman I do not like. I don't wish Susan to have anything to do with her. Do you understand?

VICCY (*with a laugh*). Really, Matron, Susan isn't eighteen—to be kept from dangerous contacts.

MATRON (*angry*). You heard what I said? This is an order.

VICCY. Well! Susan doesn't often help with treatments. She's too busy in the office, but I'll try to keep this black sheep away from her, if that's what you want. (*She is still amused.*)

MATRON. It is.

VICCY (*turning to go*). Very well. (*She is almost at door when* MATRON *calls again.*)

MATRON. Viccy.

VICCY (*turning*). Yes, Matron.

MATRON. Do you know Hugh Barrett?

VICCY. Yes, I do.

MATRON. You know that Susan has been meeting him?

VICCY. Yes.

MATRON. I want you to get rid of him.

VICCY. You what?

MATRON. I want you to get rid of him. You heard what I said. I don't wish Susan to go on meeting him. I want you to get rid of him.

VICCY. And how do you suggest I do that?

MATRON. Don't be stupid. There are ways. Contrive at a misunderstanding. Disillusion Susan in some way. I don't care what you do, so long as you break this thing up.

VICCY (icily pleasant). I see. And, may I ask—what's in it for Viccy?

MATRON. A share in this business. Susan and you and I could work together well. We'd make this the biggest health clinic in England. It would be wonderful.

VICCY. You'd stop at nothing to get your way! You'd smash up Susan's chance of happiness just so that your business arrangements should not be upset. How hard can you get?

MATRON. Don't be a fool. I want Susan's happiness, but not this way.

VICCY. You want Susan! Period! This place comes first, it always has, and it always will. Well! You can count me out. I'd like a share in this clinic. Who wouldn't? But I'm not buying it in your market.

MATRON. What do you mean?

VICCY. I mean I'm not prepared to pay your price. Do your dirty work. But let me tell you this, I think it's time Susan got the heck out of this morgue, and I'll be on the lines cheering. I'll do more. I'll tell her about these sweet little plans of yours. That should give her to think.

MATRON. Don't you dare!

VICCY. I'll do more. I shall tell Hugh and, if I know anything of the lad, he'll be up here on a white charger!

MATRON. If you say one word——

VICCY (as she goes). I know! I'm out on my neck! Fine! I'm sure tired of flappy females. I'll get me to a—a—monastery! (She exits.)

(MATRON stands looking after her for a second, then drops in a chair. She stares dumbly in front of her and then mutters.)

MATRON. What have I done? What have I done? (Her head drops into her hands as the curtain descends.)

CURTAIN.

SCENE 2.

One Hour Later.

(The stage is empty when the curtain goes up, then almost immediately RONA enters. She hesitates, looks at the telephone, then back to the door, then, making up her mind, she goes to the telephone.)

RONA. Carnstone, double four, one, five. Yes, one-five. Thank you. (She fidgets with a pen as she waits.) Hello? Hello, Helen, will you call Mr. Winstone, please? What did you say? Ah! Has he been back at all?

No? . . . Are there any letters for me? . . . Oh! I see. Yes. Yes. . . . Are there any messages? . . . I see. How are the children? . . . No, don't bother to get Nannie. I expect she's just getting them to bed. . . . Yes, yes. I'm sure you are, Helen. . . . Tell Nannie to give my love to the children. . . . I don't know—yet. . . . Very soon, I hope. . . . Yes. Goodnight, Helen.
(*She puts down the receiver and sits thinking, twisting her handkerchief in her hands.*)

(*Enter* VICCY, *carrying a book.*)

VICCY. Hello, Mrs. Winstone, you are just the person I want to see.
RONA (*dully*). Am I?
VICCY. Yes. Yes, you were supposed to come to me yesterday for some electrical massage.
RONA. I'm sorry. I forgot.
VICCY. And this morning Gloria expected you for a skin test.
RONA. Yes. I know—I—I—didn't think I'd bother.
VICCY. Not bother! Really, Mrs. Winstone!
RONA. I'm sorry. I didn't mean to be rude, but I'm—I'm a little upset and my skin test didn't seem important.
VICCY. It is important that our time schedules are kept. We are very busy and every treatment has to be most carefully planned. Now I must try to fit you in somewhere else. (*She looks through notebook.*)
RONA. Oh! Please don't bother—please don't. It doesn't matter at all—I don't want——
VICCY. You don't want any of our treatments? (*Closing notebook.*)
RONA. No.
VICCY. Not any?
RONA. No.
VICCY. Then why did you come here?
RONA. I'd heard of it, and I thought it sounded—er—peaceful.
VICCY. You do realize that our charges are based on a certain amount of treatment?
RONA. Yes, of course.   That doesn't matter.
VICCY (*with a smile*). Perhaps you may not say that when you see our bill. Don't you think you should take advantage of at least one of our treatments? What about my relaxation class? I'm sure you need that.
RONA. I don't think I shall be here long enough to—to obtain any benefit from any class.
VICCY. But Mrs. Winstone, you are booked in for a fortnight. We never undertake any treatment in less than a fortnight.
RONA (*a little wildly*). Am I?— Well, I may not stay— You can't *make* me. I don't know what I'm going to do—I—Oh, forgive me!——
(*She rushes from the room.*)

(VICCY *gazes after her for a second and then says:*)

VICCY. Well! (*She walks to fireplace and takes cigarette from box.*)

(*Enter* SUSAN. *She pulls off her head-scarf as she enters.*)

You are soon back. I thought you were meeting Hugh.

SUSAN (*sits on settee*). Yes. I met him.

VICCY. You don't sound very cheerful about it. I see no love-light in your eyes.

SUSAN. Don't!

VICCY. What's the matter, Sue? Come on, give!

SUSAN. We've quarrelled.

VICCY. Quarrelled? What over?

SUSAN. I told him that we couldn't be married yet; that we must wait for a year.

VICCY. How nice! Did you tell him why?

SUSAN. Yes, but——

VICCY. He wouldn't take it?

SUSAN. No. Oh! Surely he could wait a year for me? That isn't much to ask.

VICCY. Susan Lindy! I think you are crackers! Do you expect a man like Hugh to go on for another year as you are now? Meeting once a week if you are lucky enough to get away—sneaking out like a Victorian servant-girl to meet in the stables!

SUSAN. I know it's been difficult, but I promised my aunt for just another year. Then she'll sell this place and I'll be free.

VICCY. Like hell she will!

SUSAN. She will—she promised.

VICCY. She promised! You know this place is her whole life. Can you see her letting such a glorious racket go? Oh! Be your age, Sue. Can't you see that this is just a device to get rid of Hugh? You give him up, and in a year's time there will be no reason why everything shouldn't go on for ever.

SUSAN. Oh! Don't sneer at me, Viccy. You know as well as I do how much work there is in this place. I can't let aunt down just now. I can't. In a year's time it will be different——

VICCY. It certainly will! No Hugh, certainly no Viccy——

SUSAN. What?

VICCY. —just you and dear aunty growing old together.

SUSAN. Two dim, dedicated spinsters.

VICCY (*startled*). What did you say?

SUSAN. That's what Mrs. Heston said. She said that these kind of places are usually run by a couple of dim, dedicated spinsters.

VICCY. And by Heaven she's right! That decides it!

SUSAN. Decides what?

VICCY. Two things. First, I'm leaving.

SUSAN. Oh, no! Viccy! I couldn't stand it without you.

VICCY. You'll have to—for I'm going. I've done pretty well out of this place. I've enjoyed working with you, but your aunt! No!— I don't trust her an inch, and I'm certainly *not* going to be one of your dim and dedicated clan! Not me!

SUSAN. Viccy—stand it another year! Help me stand it. I can't go on without you.

VICCY. I'll help you to get away—I won't help you to stay.

SUSAN. I can't——

VICCY (*very seriously*). Listen, Sue! I think there is something queer going on.

SUSAN. Queer?

VICCY. Just before you came in I was talking to Matron. She seemed very upset about something. I thought at first it was because you were out with Hugh, but now I think there is something else.

SUSAN. What else could there be?

VICCY. I don't know—but it's something to do with Mrs. Heston. Have you ever heard of her before?

SUSAN. No. I don't think so.

VICCY. There's something unusual about her. I saw her this evening coming out of this room. She didn't see me. I was on the bend of the stairs, but I'll swear she had a—a *triumphant* look on her face.

SUSAN. Triumphant?

VICCY. Yes, and when I came in here it was quite obvious that your aunt was upset about something.

SUSAN. Good Heavens!

VICCY. Yes. It takes a lot to upset that old battle-axe, but I'll swear she *was*, and, what's more, she started questioning me about Mrs. Heston.

SUSAN. What do you mean?

VICCY. She wanted to know about her treatments and then asked if she'd been talking to *you*.

SUSAN. Talking to me?

VICCY. Yes. I said I didn't think so. Then she warned me to keep her away from you as she wasn't a nice person. What do you think of that?

SUSAN. How extraordinary! What does she think I am?— A tender flower?

VICCY (*laughs*). Yes—when I think of some of the types we have had here—it's rather funny!

SUSAN. Now I think of it, Mrs. Heston did seem—er—curiously familiar when I first saw her.

VICCY. What do you mean?

SUSAN. There was nothing I could pin down but I had a feeling that she was—probing, and she told me that she once worked in a clinic like this.

VICCY. Did she indeed? Now there's another thing. I wasn't going to tell you this, for I know that you are fond of your aunt, old hellion that she is—but——

SUSAN. Yes?

VICCY. Your aunt has asked me to get rid of Hugh.

SUSAN (*standing*). What?

VICCY. Oh, she's not suggesting that I bump him off, though I wouldn't put *that* past her!— No, I'm just to contrive a misunderstanding, just put a spoke in your wheel, upset Love's-Young-Dream. Anything so long as I part you and Hugh. What do you think of that?

SUSAN. I can't believe it!— Aunt wouldn't be so cruel.

VICCY. Wouldn't she? She'll fight tooth and nail to keep you.

SUSAN (*sinking to couch*). No! That's not like Aunt. I don't believe that she'd deliberately try to wreck my happiness.

VICCY. She doesn't see it like that. I think that she got crossed-in-love, or whatever it was that Victorian heroines did. Anyway, she hates men, and thinks she's saving you from a fate worse than death. (*She laughs.*)

SUSAN. What did you say?

VICCY. I asked her what was in it for me, and she generously promised, once again, a slice of this business. Nice, isn't it? Auntie, you an' little me spending the rest of our lives running this place!— Give me the fate-worse-than-death any time!

SUSAN. Did you promise to help her?

VICCY. What do you think I am? I told her to do her own dirty work, slapped in my resignation, an'—swep'—out!

SUSAN (*getting angry*). How dare she! How dare she!

VICCY. Atta boy! That's the stuff!

SUSAN. This has made up my mind for me. I thought I owed her another year, but if she can scheme like this!— Oh! It's unforgivable! I could kill her!

VICCY. Hey! Steady! Calm down. It hasn't *happened*, you know!

SUSAN. It almost has. I quarrelled with Hugh tonight, all because of her. I really thought I owed her something because she brought me up and gave me a home, but now I can see—all she wanted was a tame secretary. Someone to be at her beck and call for the rest of her life! Well! I'm through! I've finished with her! I'm going to Hugh. (*She snatches up her coat and scarf and turns to the door.*)

VICCY (*going after her*). Oh, no! You're *not*! Who do you think you are? Little Orphan Annie running off into the night?

SUSAN. Let me go!

VICCY (*pulling her back*). Come back here, you idiot! This isn't the way to do it. What do you think Hugh would do if you arrive on his door-step breathless, pantless, and penniless? You'd embarrass the dear boy no end!

SUSAN. I won't stay here.

VICCY. Oh, yes, you will. You are going to play this thing cleverly. You will wait until tomorrow, then you'll see your aunt and tell her that you—*know all*. Tell her, too, that you are going to marry Hugh and marry from here, with all the correct trappings.

SUSAN. I wouldn't——

VICCY. You *will*! Think of Hugh. He's got relatives, if you haven't. These things matter. Do you think they'd like a hole-in-the-corner marriage?

SUSAN. But——

VICCY. Remember, his practice is in this district. You must go on living here. You know this village. Do you want them to be counting their fingers for nine months?

SUSAN. Viccy!——

VICCY (*with a laugh*). They will, you know, if you rush off as you want to do.

SUSAN. Perhaps you are right.

VICCY. On the ball every time—that's Viccy! You are going to get engaged and *I'll* see it's put in *The Times*. Then you'll be married with "The Voice that breathed o'er Eden" an' champagne (probably cheap)—and I shouldn't be surprised if we can induce auntie to cough up a nice little wedding present, though I may have to twist her arm a little.

SUSAN. I do see that I mustn't do anything to harm Hugh. He's just building up his practice.

VICCY. Good girl! (*She looks at her watch.*)—Heavens! Look at the time! They'll all troop in here for their coffee at any moment.

SUSAN. I'm going— I can't——

VICCY. Look! We must keep everything as normal as possible. You know your aunt expects us to have coffee with "our guests".

SUSAN. All right. I'll just slip up and fix my face. I feel a wreck!

VICCY. Good! But you be right down, and you'll play this cool— real cool! (*She laughs.*)

SUSAN (*as she runs from the room*). Yes. I'll come back.

VICCY (*to herself, as she plumps up cushions and empties ash-trays into the fireplace*). Well! What do you know!

(*Enter* RUTH *and* TESSA *and* CLARA. CLARA *goes to chair downstage fireplace,* RUTH *to the one above.* TESSA *stands one foot on the fender.*)

TESSA (*as they enter*). So there we were at 3 a.m. stranded on Crewe Station, with about fourpence between the lot of us!

RUTH. How terrible! What an awful life!

CLARA. You've come a long way since then. (*To* VICCY.) Tessa has been telling us some of her theatrical adventures.

VICCY. How interesting! Did you start at R.A.D.A.?

TESSA. I did not. I came up the hard way. Dogsbody to the stage manager for three years and then five years in rep.

RUTH. Wonderful!

TESSA. It's been a fight, a hard fight.

VICCY. But you made it! Tessa Trevallion can pick her own parts now.

TESSA. Yes, for a while—but I don't know which is the hardest— climbing to the top, or stopping there.

CLARA. You'll stop there. I should think that you always get what you want.

TESSA (*with a smile*). Yes, I get what I want.

RUTH. Where's Mrs. Winstone? I thought she was following us.

CLARA. She said that she wanted something from her room and she'd be down later.

RUTH. I see.

TESSA. Has Mrs. Winstone been here before?

VICCY. No. This is her first visit.

TESSA. I wonder why she is here.

VICCY. For the usual reason, I suppose.

TESSA. She doesn't *look* as if she needs any of your ministrations.

VICCY. Everyone benefits from one or other of our treatments.

RUTH. That's right—too fat, too thin, dry skin or oily skin—you get us all ways, don't you, Viccy?

c

Viccy. I don't think I "get" *you* at all, Mrs. Stacey-Brown. You are the worst patient I've ever had to deal with.

Ruth. Viccy! I'm cut to the quick.

Viccy. Nonsense! You are impervious to any rebuke, and you know it.

Ruth (*laughs*). I'll reform, Viccy. Forgive me this time and I'll reform. Why, I'll even spend an hour on that damned bike.

Viccy (*quickly*). Two hours!

Ruth. Not on your life! I want to get slim—not muscle-bound.

(*They all laugh. There is a sound at the door and* Mrs. Heston *enters, followed by* Rona. Viccy *rises from settee.*)

Viccy. Do sit here, Mrs. Heston.

Mrs. H. Thank you.

(*She sits on settee.* Rona *goes to chair, side back, near table.* Viccy *sits on arm of settee.*)

I note that all the "Old Hands" come here. I can understand why. I couldn't stand the fight in the lounge.

Viccy. Fight?

Mrs. H. Polite, but deadly—for the best armchairs. (*They all laugh.*)

(*Enter* Susan)

Susan (*as she enters*). Haven't you your coffee yet?

Viccy. Don't worry. I'm sure Milly will bring some in here.

(Susan *sits on settee.*)

Mrs. H. (*to* Susan). Did you enjoy your walk?

Susan (*stiffly*). Very much, thank you.

Tessa. How very bucolic of you, to enjoy walking around here! There isn't a pavement within miles.

Susan. I detest pavements.

Tessa. I detest fields—cows are so ill-mannered—*and* badly trained.

Clara (*to* Tessa). Give me a cigarette, you urbanite.

Tessa (*as she hands box to* Clara). Don't be nasty, darling. That sounds horrid.

Ruth. Perhaps you prefer—socialite? I've seen several references to you lately in William Mickley's column.

Clara. My! What fame!

Tessa. You mustn't believe all you read in the newspapers, you know. I'm really a hard-working girl.

(Ruth *and* Clara *laugh derisively.*)

(*Protesting.*) I *am*—believe me, any running around that I do is done with one aim in view.

Ruth. And what is that?

Tessa. To help my career. Remember, publicity is the life-blood of an actress.

Clara. You don't mind what kind?

Tessa. Not a bit, so long as my name is kept before the public.

Ruth. Yes, but look here——

(*As* RUTH *speaks, the door opens and* MATRON *enters, followed by* MILLY, *who carries a large tray with coffee pot, hot milk and cups.*)

MATRON (*as she enters*). Ah! I thought you had no coffee in here. Susan, you should have come for it.

SUSAN. Sorry, Aunt.

VICCY. I was just coming.

MATRON (*to* MILLY). That's right—that table—careful now.

MILLY. Yes, Matron. (*She places tray on table at back, arranges cups, and then exits.*)

MATRON. Now, how many are there? (*She counts.*) Seven—eight.

RONA (*standing by table*). Can I help?

VICCY. Let me——

SUSAN (*moving quickly*). No. I'll help.

(VICCY *moves across to* TESSA. MATRON *and* SUSAN *pour coffee,* RONA *stands near. Their backs are to the audience.*)

TESSA (*to* VICCY). My! This is a great concession. The last time I was here I didn't get coffee.

VICCY (*smiling*). Perhaps we had a more formidable task when you were here before? Everyone doesn't get coffee, even now.

TESSA (*with a laugh*). Ah! That's true. I looked like an elephant.

VICCY. Never!

MATRON (*turning round*). Black or white?

MRS. H. Black, please.

TESSA. And for me.

MATRON. And all the others white? (*There is a murmur of assent.*)

(SUSAN *carries two cups, takes one to* RUTH, *and, keeping the other herself, returns to settee.*)

MATRON (*holding out a cup*). White?

CLARA (*as she takes it*). Thank you.

RONA (*coming forward with two cups*). Black?

MRS. HESTON (*taking a cup from over the back of settee*). Ah! Thanks.

(RONA *hands cup to* TESSA, *who steps forward to take it.*)

TESSA. Thank you, darling.

(RONA *shrinks back and returns quickly to the table, where she takes her coffee and sits in the same chair.* MATRON *holds out cup to* VICCY, *who takes it and then moves to speak to* RUTH. MATRON *picks up her own coffee and moves to chair at desk.*)

VICCY. Is that strong enough?

RUTH. Heavens! Yes. I really loath it without sugar, but I suppose I must bear it.

VICCY. You'll get to love it—eventually. (*They laugh.*)

CLARA. Where's old Lady Coulsden? Doesn't she usually honour us with her presence at this time?

MATRON. She went to bed immediately after dinner. I think she was tired.

TESSA. All that trotting up and down stairs!

(*All are sipping their coffee. No one is looking at* MRS. HESTON, *who sips hers and makes a grimace, but goes on sipping.* MATRON *is obviously ignoring her, as she turns her chair slightly and talks to* CLARA *and* TESSA.)

SUSAN (*looking across to* TESSA). Lady Coulsden isn't *made* to run upstairs, you know. It's one of her little quirks. I'm sure she enjoys her annual three weeks with us.

TESSA. I'm sure she does—the Governor's Lady, taking precedence in the drawing-room. She adores it!

CLARA. Don't be catty, Tessa.

MATRON. I am sure——

(MRS. HESTON, *during the last few sentences, has put her hand to her throat and is gasping. For a second she is not seen, then both* SUSAN *and* MATRON *notice her and spring up. All the following must go very quickly, speeches almost interlapping.*)

MATRON. Mrs. Heston. What's the matter?

SUSAN. Are you ill?

(MRS. HESTON *tries to speak, but cannot. All gather round her, except* RONA, *who stands behind settee, her face full of horror.*)

VICCY. She can't speak.

MATRON. Mrs. Heston—what's wrong? Is it your heart?

CLARA (*to* TESSA). She was all right a moment ago.

TESSA. She looks horribly ill.

SUSAN. Can I get you anything? Try to tell us.

MATRON. Are you in pain? Is it your heart?

(MRS. HESTON *makes an obvious effort, glares at* MATRON, *she points a finger at her.*)

MRS. H. You— You!—— (*The cup falls from her hand. She falls back on settee unconscious.*)

VICCY. My God! She's dead!

SUSAN (*patting* MRS. H.'s *hand*). She can't be.

MATRON (*loudly*). Nonsense! Get her a drink—quickly.

(VICCY *moves to table or cupboard backstage and quickly pours out a drink.*)

CLARA. Get the doctor, someone.

RUTH. Put her feet up.

MATRON (*to* SUSAN). Run for Doctor Soames, quickly.

(SUSAN *moves to door but stops when* RUTH *speaks.*)

RUTH (*who has picked up coffee cup and sniffed at it*). I think you are too late. Look! (*She holds out coffee cup to* MATRON, *who takes it.*)

MATRON. You can't mean?—— (*She sniffs at cup.*)

VICCY (*coming forward with drink and kneeling by* MRS. H.). Here, drink this! (*She picks up* MRS. HESTON'S *hand, then lets it drop and turns a horrified face to* MATRON.) She's dead! — Oh! My God! She's dead!

(MATRON *is still staring into the coffee cup. The tableau is held for a second. Then* RUTH *speaks.*)

RUTH. Yes—there was poison in the coffee!

QUICK CURTAIN.

ACT III.

SCENE 1.

Afternoon, the next day.

SCENE—*the same.* LADY COULSDEN *sits with her knitting in her hands but her eyes closed, in chair upstage fireplace.* TESSA *is standing near the settee, one hand on its back, vigorously swinging one leg. She is in practice costume of slacks and loose blouse. The others are in day dress.*)

TESSA (*as she swings*). One—two—one—two.

(*This continues for a few moments, then* RUTH *and* CLARA *enter.*)

RUTH (*flinging herself on to settee*). Thank goodness that's over! I'm absolutely exhausted. Give me a cigarette someone.

TESSA (*still swinging*). What tortures have you been enduring?

RUTH. I've been on that foul bike.

CLARA (*offering cigarettes*). Here you are!

RUTH (*taking cigarette*). Thanks.

CLARA (*moving to chair near desk*). For Heaven's sake, Tessa, stop swinging. What are you trying to do? Suck up to teacher?

TESSA. Idiot! I've got to get another inch off my hips and *this* is one of the pleasanter ways. (*She sits on settee near* RUTH.)

RUTH (*groaning*). Oh! My back! I'm crippled for life.

CLARA. Never mind! Now you can relax, radiated by a feeling of virtue.

RUTH. I'm radiated all right! Oooh! (*She groans again.*)

TESSA. You know, darlings, I wish you'd tell me something.

CLARA. Tell you what?

TESSA. Just what Matron thinks she's doing, trying to hush up that little—er—accident that happened last night.

RUTH (*derisively*). You are asking us?

CLARA. She knows she can't keep it secret for much longer.

TESSA. I should think not. A corpse is a mighty awkward thing to have about the house.

LADY C. (*suddenly awaking*). Corpse? What corpse? What are you talking about?

RUTH (*to the others*). Oh dear! She wasn't supposed to know.

CLARA. There's nothing to worry about, Lady Coulsden, it's just that——

LADY C. Oh! You are talking about Mrs. Heston. I told Matron she was handling the affair most foolishly.

TESSA. You what?

CLARA. We didn't know that you knew anything about it.

LADY C. Mrs. Heston's room is next to mine in the West Wing, so naturally I heard the commotion.

RUTH. What did Matron tell you?

D

LADY C. First she said that Mrs. Heston had had a heart attack and then, when I insisted on seeing her—Mrs. Heston—(after all, my dear Rupert suffered from his heart, so I do know something about it)—well, then she told me the truth!

CLARA. And swore you to silence?

LADY C. Naturally. It wouldn't do for everyone to know.

TESSA. The clamp has certainly come down.

RUTH. It had to. If all the guests knew, well, some of them might leave.

CLARA. Leave! They'd run like rabbits!

TESSA. But Matron, clever as she is, will never get away with this secrecy. It's got to come out some time.

RUTH. Has it? You forget she's got a tame doctor in the house.

CLARA. But Doctor Soames would never——

RUTH. Wouldn't she?

TESSA. I see what you mean; a nice, neat heart attack an' no questions asked! Clever stuff!

CLARA. I think she's mostly concerned with keeping it out of the papers.

RUTH. Yes. Can you see the headlines? "DEATH IN THE HEALTH CLINIC", or "THE MYSTERY OF THE COFFEE CUPS".

TESSA. "LOVE AMONGST THE LADIES" or "OO DID 'ER IN?"

LADY C. Really! I don't think you should joke over this terrible thing.

RUTH. Sorry, Lady Coulsden. We don't really think it's funny, but this place has been so gloomy that if I don't laugh I shall scream.

LADY C. I keep wondering why it was *Mrs. Heston*. None of us even knew her.

CLARA. Are you sure about that?

RUTH. What do you mean?

CLARA. Don't you remember the day that Mrs. Heston arrived, when Matron walked in and nearly fell backwards when she saw her?

RUTH. Yes, of course—and Mrs. Heston called Matron "Emilia Dale". That's the first time I knew that Matron had such a thing as a Christian name! (*She laughs.*)

TESSA. Ummm— This grows intriguing.

CLARA. And ever since Matron has quite obviously ignored Mrs. Heston.

LADY C. Perhaps Mrs. Heston has been a guest here before and hasn't got on very well with Matron. You know Matron is sometimes quite—quite——

RUTH. Fiendishly rude?— Yes, she can be—I know, but Mrs. Heston had never visited here before. I heard her saying so in the dining-room the other day.

TESSA. Curiouser, an' curiouser!

LADY C. (*rises*). I think I shall go to my room and make some tea. I have a little stove. Since this—er—happened, I feel safer with my own tea.

RUTH. But Lady Coulsden, no one would ever think of——

LADY C. Wouldn't they?

CLARA. I'm sure *you* need not worry, Lady Coulsden.

LADY C. (*moving to door*). Perhaps not, but I prefer to make my own tea and coffee now. I shall be going home tomorrow, I'm very glad to say. Can I offer either of you ladies a cup of tea?

CLARA \} (*together*). No, thank you.
RUTH / Not at the moment, thank you.

TESSA. Thanks, but I must go and change.

LADY C. (*as she exits*). Very well. I shall see you later.

RUTH. Poor old girl! She's in a proper flap. I don't believe she's due to go home until next week.

CLARA. I can't say I blame her, do you?

TESSA. No.— Less ten pounds, and another inch off my hips, and I'*d* be off. But I just haven't time to move on somewhere else. Besides, this is nothing to do with *me*. I'm keeping out of it.

CLARA. I don't see how you can keep out of it. You were there when it happened. You'll be a material witness.

TESSA (*springing up*). What!

RUTH. Then you think——

CLARA. Of course I do. Matron asked us to keep quiet for twenty-four hours and we agreed. I don't know what she hoped to achieve in that time, but one thing I am certain of is that this is a police matter and not even high-and-mighty Matron can hush it up.

TESSA. I'm not getting mixed up with the police. That's *bad* publicity. Oh, no! You can count me out. I'm off in the morning, inch or no inch.

RUTH. If the police want you, they'll bring you back.

TESSA. Oh! Hell! To get mixed up in *this* just now! Oh! It's the foulest luck! I've only got a fortnight before I sail for Australia.

CLARA. You'll be lucky!

TESSA (*furious*). I can't have this chance messed up—I can't! This is nothing to do with me. Why should I get involved? (*The usual drawl has gone. Her voice is sharp and angry.*)

RUTH. I'm afraid we're all involved, whether we like it or not.

TESSA. It doesn't matter to *you*—your life is private and you have enough money to do as you please. But I'm an *actress*; I live in the public eye and I've got a year's contract, playing lead parts. Nothing is going to imperil *that*! Nothing!

CLARA. Now, take it easy. Maybe you can get the police to keep your name out of it and I dare say you'll get away in time. I'm only saying that this *is* a *murder*. (*They both react.*) Yes, it's a nasty word, but that's what it is and as we were all in the room when it happened, then we are most certainly involved.

TESSA (*calming down*). I suppose you are right. (*She crosses to fireplace and kicks at fender.*) Oh! But it's the most hellish luck! It really is!

RUTH. I don't suppose any of us like it very much—including Mrs. Heston. (*There is a pause.*)

CLARA. I wonder who she was, and where she came from?

RUTH. She must have some relatives somewhere. I wonder what Matron has done about them.

TESSA (*who has been staring into the fire—turns*). You know, I think there has been a mistake.

CLARA. A mistake?

TESSA. Yes. I don't think that poison was meant for Mrs. Heston—someone bungled the job.

RUTH. You mean?——

TESSA. Yes. Those coffee cups got switched—the wrong person got the poison.

CLARA (*slowly*). Yes—that would have been an easy thing to do.

RUTH. There were eight of us there.

CLARA (*slowly*). You may be right, but—who was supposed to get that cup?

TESSA. I'll give you two guesses.

RUTH. You mean?——

TESSA. Matron, of course.

CLARA. Oh! No!

RUTH. Matron!

TESSA (*eagerly*). Mrs. Heston was a stranger. Oh, I know you say that you think Matron knew her, but she hasn't been near here for years, we know that. Isn't it much more likely that someone would want to bump Matron off? Personally, I think she is eminently bumpish-off-material.

RUTH. Yes, that does seem more probable.

CLARA. But— Who?

TESSA. Ah! That is the question. I can think of three suspects without even disturbing the old grey matter.

CLARA. Really, Tessa!

RUTH. Who do you mean?

TESSA (*counting on her fingers*). One, dear niece Susan; two, devoted employee Viccy; and three, old retainer Milly!

CLARA. I never heard such nonsense in my life.

RUTH. You aren't serious?

TESSA (*with a short laugh*). No. I'm not completely serious, but if you think about it, each of those three *may* have a reason for wishing to get rid of the old girl.

CLARA. So may half a dozen other people in this house.

TESSA. Yes, but those three all—as the police say—had access to the coffee.

CLARA (*looking worried*). That's true.

RUTH. You can count young Sue out. She wouldn't kill a mouse. Besides, she was very fond of her aunt.

TESSA. But fonder, I'm given to believe, of a certain local gentleman.

CLARA. That has nothing whatever to do with this case.

RUTH. Of course it hasn't.

TESSA. Perhaps not, but didn't I hear a whisper that Love's path wasn't quite smooth? Auntie was throwing rocks in the way.

CLARA. Oh! For Heaven's sake, Tessa, stop being so clever!

(TESSA *shrugs her shoulders and laughs*.)

RUTH. I know Susan is in love with young Hugh Barrett and that Matron doesn't approve, but that you should suggest that Sue could— Oh! Don't be a fool!

TESSA. Okay! Let's go to number two—the glamorous Viccy!

CLARA. No motive.

TESSA. Are you sure?

RUTH (*slowly*). Unless it was because she wanted *this* place. She told me a couple of years ago that Matron had promised to take her into partnership, but it hasn't happened yet.

CLARA. Perhaps Matron promised to leave her a part share in her will.

TESSA. Splendid! Then she and Susan could run this place as they chose, with no interference from Matron!

RUTH. Yes. I know that she and Matron don't always agree.

CLARA. This is all supposition. We haven't a *fact* to go on.

RUTH. Stop talking about it—*do*! I can't bear it. The more I think about it, the more horrible it becomes.

CLARA. I think it is time Matron told us what she is going to do.

RUTH. She asked if we would give her twenty-four hours—to make investigations.

TESSA. Those twenty-four hours are up this evening.

CLARA. I think I shall go and see her and ask for an explanation.

RUTH. And the best of British luck to you!

CLARA. Oh, *you* are coming with me.

RUTH. That I'm not!

TESSA. Don't be a coward.

RUTH. That's exactly what I am—a nice, yellowy cowardy-custard!

CLARA. You are coming just the same. I want your moral support.

RUTH. But I——

TESSA. She can't eat you!

RUTH. No! Just freeze me solid!

CLARA (*pulling her up*). Come on up!

RUTH. No!

CLARA. Come on. Let's beard the lion.

RUTH. I hate lions.

(SUSAN *enters. She carries some papers.*)

SUSAN. Hello there! What's the argument?

CLARA. I want Mrs. Stacey-Brown to come with me to see Matron.

SUSAN. I see.

RUTH. But I— (*She looks at* SUSAN.) Oh! All right, I'll come.

CLARA (*to* SUSAN). Where is Matron?

SUSAN. In her office, I think.

CLARA. Good.

RUTH (*as they move to door*). Well—be it on your own head——

(*They exit.*)

(TESSA *stretches her arms above her head and yawns.* SUSAN *goes to desk, sits and begins to look at papers.*)

TESSA. I must go and change. I suppose tea will be here in a moment.

SUSAN (*not looking at* TESSA). I have asked Milly to serve tea only in the lounge today.

TESSA. Have you? Seeking a little solitude, eh?

SUSAN. This *is* my office and I have work to do.

TESSA. Fine, darling. I can take a hint. I'll make myself scarce.

(SUSAN *doesn't reply but bends over her papers.* TESSA *reaches door and then turns back.*)

I think I'd better tell you that I'm leaving in the morning.

SUSAN (*swinging round*). Leaving? But you are booked for another ten days.

TESSA. Sorry, my sweet, but my agent calls, an' when an agent calls, I run. (*She exits quickly.*)

(SUSAN *turns to desk, and puts her head in her hands. There is a short pause and* VICCY *enters.*)

VICCY (*as she enters*). Can you let me have—? (*She sees* SUSAN.) Why, Sue, what's the matter?

(SUSAN *shakes her head, but doesn't reply.*)

Come on, Sue. Things aren't as bad as *that.*

SUSAN. They are! Everything has gone wrong. I've lost Hugh, quarrelled with my aunt, then there was that dreadful thing last night—an' now everyone is leaving.

VICCY (*sharply*). Leaving? Who is leaving?

SUSAN. Lady Coulsden for one, and now Tessa Darke says she is going in the morning.

VICCY. That's not everyone. I, for one, will be glad to see the back of old Lady Coulsden. And as for Tessa Darke, I'll deal with her. Where is she? (*She moves towards the door.*)

SUSAN. It's no good. You can't make her stay if she doesn't want to.

VICCY. Can't I? Perhaps not, but I'll make it darned unpleasant for her.

SUSAN. She's furious. She doesn't want to get mixed up in this—this accident.

VICCY. She's in it, and she can't run away. For once in her life, Tessa Darke will have to do as she's told.

SUSAN. What's happening, Viccy? My aunt won't tell me a thing. All she says is—"Carry on as though nothing has happened". What does she hope to do?

VICCY. I don't know. There's something mighty mysterious going on. I saw her this afternoon and told her that she hadn't a hope of hushing this thing up.

SUSAN. What did she say?

VICCY. She said we must wait until this evening when she wanted to see all of us together—that is, all of those who were here last night—then she would have something to tell us.

SUSAN. I don't understand it.

VICCY. Neither do I. What's she trying to do?— Reconstruct the crime as they do in thrillers?

SUSAN. It seems like it.

VICCY. I think she's got some mad idea of finding the poisoner *before* she gets the police on the job.

SUSAN. It must be that.

(*Enter* MILLY *carrying tea-tray.*)

MILLY. I saw you come in, Miss, and I thought you'd like some tea here—quiet-like.

SUSAN. Milly! You are an angel.

MILLY. I've put *all* the other tea in the lounge, an' I've told everyone, very loud, that you was busy.

(MILLY *puts tray on coffee-table and sits on settee, and pours out.*)

VICCY. I'm glad to see I'm allowed a cup.

MILLY. You are.

VICCY. Milly, has Matron or Doctor said anything to you about this beastly business?

MILLY. No. What could they say? Here you are. (*She hands tea.*)

SUSAN. Thanks.

VICCY (*taking tea*). Lovely!

MILLY. Don't see as 'ow they can hush it up much longer. Got a corpse on their 'ands, they 'ave.

SUSAN. Oh! Don't!

VICCY. Suppose she died of heart failure?— That's a nice convenient death to have.

MILLY. Eh, Miss, that's what I've been thinking. Let us out, wouldn't it?

SUSAN. Milly! My aunt would never suggest such a thing. I know she wouldn't.

VICCY. Your aunt would do almost anything to protect the good name of this place.

SUSAN. Oh! Why did that woman come here? And who could want to kill her?

MILLY. 'Oo indeed! (*Moves to door.*)

VICCY. Milly! You know something!

MILLY. That I don't, Miss.

SUSAN. Then you suspect?

MILLY (*as she exits*). P'raps I do— p'raps I don't. Drink your tea, Miss, before it gets cold.

SUSAN. Isn't Milly the most exasperating?——

VICCY. Milly is deep. She's been with your aunt for years, hasn't she?

SUSAN. Oh, yes! For ever—before I was born—I know that. I wonder what she was hinting?

VICCY. I think it's quite plain. She knows that your aunt knew Mrs. Heston before she came here, and I think she suspects——

SUSAN. Suspects what?

VICCY. That your aunt had reason to hate Mrs. Heston, hate her so much that she could kill her.

SUSAN (*in horror*). Oh! No! No!

VICCY. Why not? Don't you think your aunt is capable of killing, if she thought it necessary?

SUSAN. No. I won't believe it. I won't.

VICCY. Well!— Someone did it!

SUSAN. Not my aunt. It wasn't *her*. It was an accident. It must have been.

VICCY. It wasn't an accident. Someone put poison in that cup. Someone wanted—someone to die.

SUSAN. Oh! It's so horrible.

(*Enter* RONA WINSTONE. *She carries a coat over her arm, and a small suit-case. She looks upset and unhappy.*)

VICCY. Mrs. Winstone? What is the matter?

RONA (*vaguely*). I'm going away.

VICCY. Going away?— But you can't. There isn't another train today.

RONA (*taking no notice of* VICCY). I must go away. I wanted to go before, but there's nowhere to go.

SUSAN (*going to her*). Mrs. Winstone, what is wrong?

RONA. Where do you go when there's nowhere to go? Tell me that?

VICCY. Mrs. Winstone, you can't go off like this. Leave it until tomorrow, then I can arrange a car for you.

RONA. No! No! I can't stay here any longer. I can't stay here with her.

SUSAN. With whom? What do you mean?

RONA. I must go. Let me go.

VICCY (*firmly*). I think you must stay for another day or two, Mrs. Winstone. You were there last night, and I think the Police——

(*Before she can finish or say any more,* RONA *spins round and, with a strangled cry, says:*)

RONA. Police!— Oh!— No! (*She drops to the floor in a dead faint.*)

CURTAIN.

SCENE 2.

After dinner, four hours later.

SCENE, *the same, but a lamp on the desk is alight.* RUTH *and* CLARA *are sitting on settee.* TESSA *is sitting on arm of chair upstage fireplace.* TESSA *is smoking. They are all in informal evening dress.*

RUTH (*to* TESSA). Was she icy? My dear! I was frozen to the floor. It was that particular kind of polite iciness which Matron specializes in. You know.

TESSA. Did you get anything definite out of her?

CLARA. Not much. Things were being investigated; she hoped to be able to make a statement soon, etc., etc.

RUTH. She trusted to our sense of—er—delicacy that we would not divulge (yes, that was the word) anything to the other guests. Personally, I'm for a spot of divulging all round.

CLARA. I told Matron quite firmly that if I wasn't given a satisfactory explanation soon, I should leave.

RUTH. Mrs. Winstone said she was going today. Have you seen her?

TESSA. She avoids me as though I have a particularly nasty kind of leprosy.

RUTH. She's queer. When I asked her this morning if she was going home, she gave me a haunted kind of look and said: "No! No! I couldn't," and then she bolted.

CLARA. Viccy thinks she's crackers.

RUTH. No. She isn't; she's just unhappy about something. She keeps telephoning her home and having long conversations with "Nannie" about the children.

TESSA. Why the heck doesn't she go home to them if she's so worried? These neurotic women make me tired. The rich and beautiful Mrs. Ralph Winstone—haven't you seen her in the *Tatler*?

CLARA. I thought I knew her face.

TESSA. You've seen it often enough, she's usually swathed in mink, or on the terrace, complete with nicely posed family and the dogs.

RUTH. I think you know more about her than you admit.

TESSA. I don't. I've never seen her before.

CLARA. You sound as though you hate her.

TESSA. Not her exactly, but her type. They get born into the right bed, so everything is handed to them on a silver plate. They never have to fight for anything, they *expect* life to be kind. They *expect* love, riches and what have you, as their right.

RUTH. And when they find something missing they can't fight.

TESSA. Can't or won't—it comes to the same thing.

CLARA. I'm sorry for them. They have no armour, and we all need some protective armour in this world.

TESSA. Yes. I grew mine young. I had to.

RUTH. And you are going to see that there are no cracks?

TESSA. That's right. "What's in it for Tessa?" You'll find that imprinted on my heart—my stony heart. (*She laughs.*)

(*There is a sound in the hall, and* SUSAN *and* VICCY *enter.*)

VICCY (*to* RUTH). Hello there! Who missed a massage period today?

RUTH. You were so busy, I thought you would be grateful to me.

VICCY (*goes to fireplace, sits in chair downstage, takes cigarette*). I was, but you mustn't do it. You are paying for it, you know.

RUTH. Oh! That.

SUSAN (*sits at desk*). Did you see Matron?

CLARA. We did. Ruth is just recovering from frostbite.

SUSAN. Nonsense!

RUTH. It's true, but she did tell us that she hopes to be able to explain everything this evening.

VICCY. Yes. We are going to get everyone together and try to find out exactly what happened.

RUTH (*happily*). Ah! I know. Reconstructing the crime. Oh, goody!

SUSAN. I think you must take this thing seriously, Mrs. Stacey-Brown.

RUTH (*contrite*). Sorry, but I've never been concerned in a crime before. I think it's rather exciting.

TESSA. What a pity we haven't a handsome detective-inspector. They always look such pets.

CLARA. I cannot conceive that Matron really thinks she can hush this

E

thing up. A dead woman is a mighty inconvenient thing to have about the house.

VICCY. I think Matron knows what she's doing.

CLARA. I've no doubt of *that*.

RUTH (*quickly*). Let's leave it. I've a feeling that there's something pretty queer coming up.

TESSA. Queer! I think you are *all* potty.

SUSAN. I'm beginning to think so myself.

TESSA. Perhaps it's catching. By the way, speaking of pottiness, where is Mrs. Winstone?

RUTH. Yes. She was here at the fatal moment.

SUSAN. Was she at dinner?

RUTH. Yes, sitting by herself, as usual, in the corner near the door.

CLARA. I think she sits there because it's near the telephone in the hall.

VICCY. Near the telephone?

CLARA. Yes. She seems to spend her life waiting for a telephone call that never comes.

SUSAN. How terrible!

TESSA. How daft!

VICCY. I'll go and see if I can find her. (*Exit* VICCY. *There is a short pause.*)

RUTH. I rather feel as though I am about to be tried.

TESSA (*lightly*). Yes. Where were you on the night of the fifth? Have you any odd arsenic or prussic acid tucked away in your bra?

CLARA. Shut up, Tessa. We're all feeling a bit scratchy.

TESSA. Sorry, darling. I was only trying to ease the tension or what have you.

SUSAN. Please let us try to keep calm. It won't be for very much longer. (*There is a sound from the hall.*) Ah! Here's Matron!

(*Enter* MATRON, *followed by* MILLY, *carrying a tray of coffee.*)

MATRON. Put the tray on that table, Milly. (*She indicates table as before.*)

MILLY. Okay.

MATRON (*looking round*). Now, are we all here?

SUSAN. Viccy has gone to fetch Mrs. Winstone.

MATRON. I see.

CLARA. May I ask?——

MATRON. Please, Miss Fanton, do not ask questions just yet.

CLARA. But— Oh! Very well.

MATRON (*to* MILLY). That will do, Milly.

MILLY. I wants to stay, please.

MATRON. You were not here at—er—during the time, Milly. I see no reason why you should stay.

MILLY. All the same, Matron, I wants to. I feel I've got a n'interest, being with you all these years. (*The last sentence is said very firmly; a long look passes between* MATRON *and* MILLY.)

MATRON. Very well, but stay back there. (*She waves her hand to the back of the room.* MILLY *nods and goes backstage to window seat.*) Now, I would like you all to sit where you were last evening.

TESSA. I was over here, standing. (*She moves to fireplace.*)

CLARA (*moving*). I was in this chair. (*To chair up fireplace.*)

SUSAN (*to settee*). I was here and Viccy was at the back, near the table.

MATRON. That's right. I sat here at the desk.

(*Enter* VICCY *and* RONA.)

VICCY. Now I think we are all here. (*She moves to table back.*)

MATRON. Ah! Mrs. Winstone, will you sit where you did before?

(RONA, *who looks very ill, nods and moves to chair at back.*)

Now, ladies, I believe that we are seated just as we were last night.

TESSA (*cheerfully*). Except that Mrs. Heston was on the settee.

MATRON (*giving her a look of dislike*). Exactly. Now, as you know, one of our guests was poisoned, the poison being given in the coffee cup.

(*They all nod.*)

I've called you here tonight because I believe that together we can find out who administered that poison.

TESSA. Don't you *know*?

MATRON (*sharply*). No. I do not, Mrs. Darke, otherwise I should not be here.

RUTH. Who poured that coffee?

MATRON. I poured some of it, and Viccy the rest.

SUSAN. I poured some of the milk.

CLARA. Well, I didn't move from here.

RUTH. Yes, you did You went over to the table.

CLARA. Oh!— Surely Viccy gave me a cup?

VICCY. No. I don't think I did.

MATRON. I think it was I who handed your cup to you.

CLARA. Shows how you can get confused!

SUSAN. I took a cup to Mrs. Stacey-Brown. Didn't I?

RUTH. Yes that's right.

SUSAN. Then I sat down with mine.

TESSA. Mrs. Winstone handed me mine.

MATRON (*to* RONA). Is that so?

RONA. Yes. Then I took my own and sat down.

MATRON. I remember taking two cups; one I handed to Miss Fanton, the other I kept for myself.

VICCY. This is very queer. One of us handed that coffee to Mrs. Heston. Now, who was it? (*She looks round and there is a silence.*)

TESSA (*cheerfully*). Not getting very far, are we? Perhaps the poison was in the cup *before* it came into the room?

MATRON. What are you suggesting?

MILLY (*springing up*). That it wasn't! *I* made that coffee!

VICCY. Did anyone help you?

MILLY. Only Matron. She was putting the cups out while I made the coffee.

(*There is a tense pause.*)

TESSA (*softly*). Only Matron.

MATRON. This is ridiculous! Do you think I'd be such a fool as to kill one of my own guests in sight of three others? Do you think I'd do such a thing here—where any scandal, any breath of even suspicion would ruin my business? Don't be idiotic.

SUSAN. Of course no one would believe such a thing, Aunt. Besides, what would be the motive?

VICCY. Perhaps you didn't intend to kill her? Just enough poison to keep her out of the way, to keep her from talking.

MATRON. Why should I do that?

VICCY. I suggest you ask Milly.

MATRON (*swinging round*). Milly! What have you been saying?

MILLY (*innocently*). Nothing, Matron.

VICCY. Who *is* Mrs. Heston? Did you know her before she came here?

(*There is a pause.*)

MATRON. Yes. I knew Erica Heston many years ago.

TESSA. Ah! The past returns.

VICCY. Did you have any reason to hate her?

MILLY (*before* MATRON *can speak*). That she didn't! I know that.

MATRON (*to* MILLY). You keep out of this.

MILLY. If you ask me, Matron, you'll 'ave to tell them.

MATRON. Will you keep quite, Milly.

MILLY. Well, you can see what they're thinking. Much better tell 'em the truth. The Lord knows it can't matter now.

(*As* MILLY *speaks the door opens and* MRS. HESTON *stands in the doorway. They all swing round.*)

MRS. H. Yes, the truth, Emilia! Will you tell them or shall I?

(*There is an instant reaction from them all, exclamations overlapping each other. They all spring up, except* RONA.)

VICCY. Well— I'm!——

SUSAN. Mrs. Heston!

TESSA. But you are——

RUTH. Holy smoke!

CLARA. Mrs. Heston! Then you aren't——

(*Only* RONA *does not speak. She puts her hand to her mouth and gazes in amazement at* MRS. HESTON. MRS. HESTON *moves forward, obviously enjoying the sensation she has caused.*)

MRS. H. No, Miss Fanton. I'm not dead.

SUSAN. But we thought——

MRS. H. I know you did.

VICCY (*turning to* MATRON). Is this your idea of a joke?

MRS. H. The report of my death was, shall we say, greatly exaggerated, but it wasn't Matron's idea to play this trick on you. It was *mine*.

TESSA (*angrily*). Then let me tell you I don't think it amusing.

RUTH. Neither do I.

CLARA. You've given us a very bad twenty-four hours.

SUSAN. I think it was unforgivable. Aunt, how *could* you do this?

MRS. H. Your aunt couldn't do anything else. I insisted.

VICCY. *You* insisted! Who are you to upset us and our guests like this?

Mrs. H. (*sweetly*). I'm the one that got poisoned. Remember?

Susan. Yes, but——

Mrs. H. Oh! I was poisoned all right. Doctor Soames can confirm that. Fortunately, the poisoner slipped up. I wasn't given quite enough of the stuff. I was very ill for some hours, but, as you see, I'm still here, annoying as that may be for someone.

Ruth. But why the pretence?

Mrs. H. I wanted to give the person who slipped that poison in my coffee a bad time. After all—she gave me one.

Viccy. Then you don't know?——

Mrs. H. No. I don't, but I've a pretty shrewd idea, and that's why I insisted on this gathering tonight. I'm going to make the murderess confess, and tell you why she did it——Yes, confess in front of you all. (*Her tone is bitter and she looks at* Matron, *who drops weakly on to the settee.*)

Milly. You always was a trouble-maker—never trusted you, I didn't! Knew as soon as I saw you that you was up to no good.

Mrs. H. And you were quite right, Milly, so now will you please shut up and mind your own business. (*This sentence begins politely but ends angrily.*)

Matron. It's no good, Milly, you can't help me now.

Susan. What *is* all this? And who are you?

Mrs. H. That is what I want your aunt to tell you.

Matron (*almost pleadingly*). Erica, I'll tell Susan. I see I have no alternative, but let us leave it until later. Surely it has nothing to do with the matter in hand.

Mrs. H. Hasn't it? I think it most decidedly *has*. I was poisoned, here in this room. No one here knows me, except *you*, and *you* have a very good reason for wishing me out of the way.

Viccy. What reason?

Susan. You must be mad to suggest such a thing.

Mrs. H. Perhaps you will judge *that* better when you know why your aunt wanted me out of the way.

Clara (*after a quick look at* Tessa *and* Ruth). Matron, would you like us to go?

Mrs. H. *I* should like you to stay.

Matron. It doesn't matter. I can see Mrs. Heston insists upon having her pound of flesh.

Mrs. H. I *do*. I came here with a straightforward proposal to put in front of you. I didn't expect to get bumped off! Now—I'm going to make *you* suffer.

Viccy. What proposal was that?

Matron. She tried to blackmail me into taking her into partnership.

Susan ⎱
Viccy ⎰ (*together*). *What?*

Mrs. H. Blackmail is a nasty word, but murder is a worse one. Are you going to tell them—or shall I?

Matron (*rising*). I'll tell them everything. I don't think it matters now.

MRS. H. (*sitting*). Well, get on with it.

(MATRON *walks to the centre of the stage and, after a moment's hesitation, speaks.*)

MATRON. I knew Erica Heston many years ago. Although only a little older than I, she came to be a companion to me. I had no mother, and my father, a rich business man, had very little time for me. We got on very well together until I met and fell in love with a young man. Erica was, I think, a little jealous——

MRS. H. Nonsense!

MATRON (*taking no notice of her, continues*)—and she sided with my father, who did not approve of the man and forbade me to meet him. In despair I ran away to Gretna Green. (*She pauses.*)

SUSAN. Poor Aunt!

MRS. H. Go on!

MATRON. I knew nothing of having to wait for three weeks to establish residential qualifications. I thought we could get married immediately. Of course, my father came after me, and the young man proved a very broken reed. A few threats from my father and he ran away. I was brought back in disgrace and that was that.

SUSAN. Did you never see him again?

MATRON. Never, but a month later I knew I was going to have a child.

(*Instant reaction from them all.*)

SUSAN. What!

VICCY. So that's——

MATRON (*holding up her hand*). No. Let me continue. I was frantic with fear. I had no one to turn to, until at last I was forced to tell— (*she turns and looks at* MRS. HESTON) her. She helped me to get away, persuading my father that I needed a holiday. With Milly, we went to Italy, and there I waited for my baby.

MRS. H. Your unwanted baby!

MATRON (*calmly*). Yes, my unwanted baby. I had no idea what I would do after it was born, but that problem was solved when, suddenly and unexpectedly, I heard that my father had died from coronary thrombosis. (*She pauses again.*)

MRS. H. Come along, finish the story.

MATRON. There isn't much more to tell. I had my baby, then left it with Erica Heston whilst I went back to England to settle my affairs. My father had left me a good deal of money, so now I was free to do as I liked. I had intended to have my baby adopted, but, once I saw her, I knew I could never do that. I lived in Italy for some months and then came back to England with—my niece.

(*All react.*)

SUSAN (*springing up*). What?

MATRON. Yes, Susan. You are my daughter.

SUSAN. But— Oh! It isn't true?

MRS. H. It's true all right. *You* were the little mistake.

MATRON (*fiercely*). Be quiet!

SUSAN. Oh!— Oh! I don't know what to say. Why didn't you tell me?

MATRON. I've wanted to, oh! so many times, but I'd built up such a structure of lies I couldn't find a way to break them down.

SUSAN. You—my Mother! Oh!

VICCY (to SUSAN). Sit down, Sue. Take it easy.

TESSA. So this was the blackmail?

MATRON. Yes. Erica Heston was helpful to me in those days and, when it was over, I paid her a pretty large sum of money for her services.

MRS. H. You paid to get rid of me.

MILLY. You wanted to go—couldn't wait, you couldn't, to go off on the splash. *SPREE*

MATRON. I never saw her again until she came to this house two days ago.

CLARA. She came to threaten to expose you?

TESSA (with a laugh). Is this all? Did you let yourself get blackmailed over a baby you had twenty-eight years ago? It's all such aeons ago, it couldn't matter a hoot by now.

MATRON. It mattered, and still matters to me. Remember, I have, over the years, built up a high reputation.

RUTH. Yes, I can understand that.

VICCY (to MRS. H.). Pleasant type, aren't you?

MRS. H. (cheerfully). No, not very, but I've had to learn to look after myself.

VICCY. Obviously!

MRS. H. (fiercely). Yes, and I've done it pretty well, until I came to this place—and almost got murdered.

(There is a silence.)

MRS. H. Do you have to ask now who tried to do it?

SUSAN (turning to MATRON). No— No— I know you couldn't do such a thing.

MATRON. No, Sue, I didn't. I know that suspicion points to me, but I didn't do it.

MRS. H. I think you did.

MATRON. No. I decided to buy you off.

MRS. H. What?

MATRON. Not with a partnership in this place, but I'd help you to start your own clinic somewhere.

MRS. H. Will you really?

MATRON. I said I *had* decided. Now that you have forced me to humiliate myself in this way, why, you have nothing to sell any more. Have you?

MRS. H. But I——

SUSAN. I think you have over-reached yourself, Mrs. Heston.

VICCY. Yes, clever, but not quite clever enough.

MRS. H. You think so?

TESSA. If you ask me, you hadn't many cards in your hands to begin with, and what you *did* have you've overplayed, always a bad mistake.

MRS. H. I don't think I asked your opinion.

MILLY. No, an' you didn't ask mine but I agrees. No one but Matron 'ere would have cared a brass farthing about sich a thing anyway.

MATRON (*to* MRS. H.). If you are satisfied with what you have done, perhaps you will now leave this house?

MRS. H. (*furious*). Leave this house? Aren't you forgetting one thing? I was *poisoned*! Do you think I'm going to let you or anyone else get away with *that*? I'm going to call the police. This case will make headlines tomorrow.

(*She strides to the telephone. As she puts her hand on it,* VICCY'S *hand comes down over hers.*)

VICCY. I don't think I should call the police, Mrs. Heston.

MRS. H. You don't? Well, you think again. (*She tries to push* VICCY'S hand away.)

VICCY. No. *Blackmail* has a nasty sound.

MRS. H. Not so nasty as murder. (*She tries to wrench her hand from the telephone.*)

VICCY. But no one *was* murdered.

MRS. H. I was—almost.

VICCY. Almost, but not quite.

MRS. H. Are you going to let someone get away with it?

MATRON. Of course not, Mrs. Heston. I bitterly regret what happened to you. I have already apologized and I do so again, and I assure you that *I*, more than anyone else, wish to solve this mystery.

MRS. H. (*sitting down*). Then you'd better get on with it. That's all I can say.

MATRON (*softly to* SUSAN, *who has been sitting with her head in her hands*). Don't worry, Sue, we'll talk this out later, but I'm glad you know at last—very glad.

SUSAN. So am I.

TESSA (*lighting a cigarette*). Now this interesting confession series is over, I suggest that we get down to the thing that really matters.

RUTH. Yes, who did it? And, equally important—why ?

CLARA. Matron, I feel I must tell you this. It has been suggested (*she looks at* TESSA) that perhaps that poison went to the wrong person.

MATRON. What do you mean?

CLARA. That it may have been meant—for *you*.

VICCY ⎫ (*together*). Well! Blow me down!
SUSAN ⎭   Oh! No!

MATRON. Indeed! And were there any suggestions as to who wished me out of the way?

RUTH (*hurriedly*). No, no! Of course not.

TESSA (*to* CLARA). Come on, little George Washington, tell them.

CLARA (*uncomfortably*). I—I can't.

MRS. H. I'll make two guesses. It was either Viccy, or dear daughter Susan.

(VICCY *and* SUSAN *spring up and speak, almost together.*)

VICCY. What damned nonsense! Why should *I* want to kill Matron?

SUSAN. How dare you make such a suggestion!

MRS. H. I don't think I *did* say it, I just guessed what these others probably said.

VICCY (*to* RUTH *and* CLARA). Did you really think that either Susan or I could do such a thing?

RUTH. No, but who *did* do it?

CLARA. I think *you* are quite capable of it, given sufficient motive.

VICCY. Thank you. Thank you very much!

CLARA (*continuing*). —But I'm sure Susan is quite incapable of such an action.

SUSAN. You all know that I have always loved my aunt—er—mother.

MATRON. "Aunt" will do, Susan, for the time being.

TESSA. I'm sick of this merry-go-round. I suggest we go—Eeny—meeny—miny—mo! (*She points all round until her finger comes to rest on* RONA.)

RONA (*in a strangled voice*). No!

(*They all turn to look at* RONA.)

TESSA. You—Mrs. High-Society-Ralph-Winstone, you've been very quiet. Can't we have a few true confessions from you?

RONA. Leave me alone!

MRS. H. (*suddenly*). I remember now—*you* handed me that coffee.

(*They all react.*)

MATRON. Are you sure?

MRS. H. That I am.

TESSA. Yes. She picked up two cups, gave one to Mrs. Heston and the other to me.

RONA. I didn't! I didn't!

TESSA. But you *did*. I remember being almost struck dumb with the look you gave me.

MATRON. You certainly did hand round some coffees.

MRS. H. (*going round to* RONA). Now, why in Heaven's name did you want to get rid of *me*? What had I done to *you*?

RONA. Nothing! Nothing! I didn't do it.

VICCY. You were the only one who handled that cup.

RONA. No! No!

MATRON. Mrs. Winstone—why did you poison that coffee?

RONA. Leave me alone! I'm going to my room. (*She starts to move.*)

MRS. H. (*darting in front of her*). No you don't! You stay here until we get the truth out of you.

TESSA. Come on, come clean! Why did you want Mrs. Heston out of the way?

RONA (*she is facing them from backstage centre*). I didn't— Not Mrs. Heston.

TESSA (*quickly*). Then it was someone else?

MATRON. Who was that poison meant for, Mrs. Winstone?

(RONA *does not reply.*)

MATRON. You must tell us.

RONA. I didn't mean—— (*She stops again.*)

TESSA. My God! I've just seen it! She got the cups mixed. That poison was meant for *me*. (*She rushes to* RONA, *seizes her, and begins shaking her*.) That was it, wasn't it? You wanted to kill *me*. Come on—tell the truth, or I'll shake it out of you!

RONA. Yes, yes. It was for you!

TESSA (*in a fury, still shaking her*). You damned murderess! Try to kill *me*, would you? I should have known it—you weak-kneed little slut! Can't fight, so you poison!

VICCY (*springing to pull* TESSA *away from* RONA). That's enough! Stop it!

TESSA. Stop it! She tried to kill me! That poison was meant for *me!*

VICCY (*pushing* TESSA *on to the settee*). Well, you didn't get it, so shut up for the moment.

(RONA, *who is weeping bitterly, sways.* SUSAN *and* CLARA *run to her.*)

SUSAN. Come and sit down, Mrs. Winstone.

(*They help her to chair near fireplace.*)

TESSA. Let me——

MATRON (*almost shouting*). Will you all be quiet, please.

(*There is a sudden silence.*)

MATRON. Mrs. Winstone! Try to pull yourself together. You must tell us why you did this terrible thing.

RONA (*lifting her head*). Because she's an evil woman. She deserves to die.

TESSA. What have I done to you?

RONA. Taken my husband, broken up my home—broken my heart. (*She weeps.*)

(TESSA *makes a derisive noise.*)

MATRON. Is this true?

TESSA. No. Oh! I had a little run around with Ralph, but that was ages ago. I haven't seen him for months.

RONA. You took him away from me.

TESSA. Oh! Grow up, can't you! You can't "take" a man unless he is waiting to be "taken". I went around with your husband. It got me mentioned in the society papers, but it didn't last long. I soon realized that he was no good for *me*. He wasn't even interested in the theatre. So I dropped him.

RONA. It isn't true.

TESSA. It *is*— I never wanted him much, and I don't want him now. I'm off to Australia in a fortnight. What would I do with Mr. Ralph Winstone, M.P., on tour?

RONA. Then why does he stay in Town? Why am I left alone?

TESSA. I should ask him. You may get a dusty answer, but I should ask.

SUSAN (*going to* RONA). You know, Mrs. Winstone, your husband is a very important politician. I'm always reading about him in the papers. Don't you think he may just be very busy?

RONA. Perhaps. Oh—I don't know—I've been nearly frantic with worry. I hardly know what I've been doing these last few days.

MATRON. Did you come here with the intention of killing Mrs. Darke?

RONA (*amazed*). Of course not! I didn't know her. Until I met her here I'd never seen her before.

MATRON. But the poison—you had that?

RONA. Yes. It was for myself.

MATRON (*outraged*). What! You intended to commit suicide, *in my house*!

VICCY. That would have been lovely.

MRS. H. Nearly as bad as murder!

RONA. I'm sorry, but I did. I kept waiting for a call from my husband. You see, I'd written him a letter, telling him what I was going to do. When he didn't call, I felt that everything was finished for me. I didn't care what happened any more.

RUTH. Poor dear.

TESSA (*still angry*). Poor dear! Is that all you can say? She tried to poison me—and all you can say is—poor dear!

RONA. I acted on an impulse. I hardly knew what I was doing. I was sorry immediately I'd done it, and when I thought I'd killed Mrs. Heston Oh! (*She puts her head in her hands.*) It was terrible!

MATRON. I think we've had enough of this. I suggest you go to bed, Mrs. Winstone.

MILLY. An' about time, too. Come on, deary. I'll help you. (*She goes to RONA.*)

RONA (*standing—to* MRS. H.). I'm sorry, so sorry. Do try to forgive me.

MRS. H. I must say I'm glad you weren't more successful—but it's all right. Just try to forget it. I shall.

RONA. Thank you—thank you so much. If there's anything I can do——

MRS. H. Well now, there may be, but go to bed now. I'll see you again tomorrow.

VICCY. Come on, Mrs. Winstone.

SUSAN. I'll go with them.

(SUSAN *and* MILLY *,helping* RONA, *move towards door.*)

MATRON. Try to sleep. Things will look different in the morning.

TESSA (*sneering*). And remember you've got out of this darned lightly. But then, you are Mrs. Ralph Winstone! That makes a difference!

(RONA *gives her a look of disgust and* SUSAN, MILLY *and* RONA *exit.*)

MATRON (*briskly*). I apologize again to you all for all this unpleasantness, but I suggest that now it is over we try to forget it. I'm sure you agree with me when I say that it would be most unwise to let this matter go any further—for all our sakes.

CLARA. Of course.

RUTH. Yes. Let's forget the whole thing.

MRS. H. Easy, isn't it? Forget the whole thing, she says! Let me tell you that *I* had about twelve hours that will take a lot of forgetting.

MATRON (*icily*). I'm sure we can find *some* way for erasing those memories. (*She turns to* TESSA.) I'm sure *you* don't want to be involved in any scandal just now, do you?

TESSA (*reluctantly*). No—but I'd like——

VICCY. To punish Mrs. Winstone?——

TESSA (*violently*). Yes——When I think——

VICCY (*quickly*). Perhaps this will teach you to keep your hands off other people's husbands!

TESSA. How dare you!

VICCY. Mrs. Winstone did wrong, but I can understand it. If you torment a kitten long enough you find the tiger.

MATRON. I think it would be as well if you left in the morning, Mrs. Darke.

TESSA. Leave! Let me tell you I can't get out of this place quickly enough.

VICCY. Good! I never did like petty thieves.

TESSA. Thieves! Well—I'm damned! What are you doing? Setting up a court of morals? (*Moving to door—to* MATRON.) I should advise you to watch this—this underhand schemer, and your illegitimate daughter, or she may follow her mother's example! (*She rushes from room.*)

RUTH. Well!

CLARA. How rude!

MATRON (*smiling*). It doesn't matter. I don't think I care any more what people say or think.

VICCY. What a spiteful little bitch!

CLARA. Come along, Ruth. I think we'd better go to bed.

RUTH. Yes. (*To* VICCY.) I suppose you will have me on various tortures in the morning?

MATRON. Then you are not leaving us?

RUTH. Of course not.

CLARA. Why should we leave? I've another two weeks booked.

MATRON. Thank you both. You've been very patient and I'm most grateful to you.

RUTH (*to door*). Don't worry, Matron. These things are soon forgotten.

CLARA (*following her*). Of course they are. Good night, Matron, good night, Viccy.

MATRON. Good night.

RUTH. See you in the morning.

VICCY. Will you. Good night.

(RUTH *and* CLARA *exit.*)

(*There is a short silence as* MATRON *moves to chair near fireplace and sits, pressing her hands to her face in a tired gesture.* VICCY *moves to desk and takes cigarette from box and stands, leaning on desk.* MRS. HESTON *sits on settee.*)

MRS. H. Well, Emilia, what now?

MATRON. Yes, indeed. That is the question.

VICCY. I suggest that the sooner you get out of here the better.

MRS. H. How kind of you! I never intended to stay long.

MATRON. Just long enough to get what you wanted.

MRS. H. You are dead right, and I seem to have made rather a mess of *that*. I was so furious about that poison. I didn't think——

VICCY. You certainly didn't!

MATRON. Yes. I see I do owe you something by way of compensation for those bad twelve hours.

MRS. H. Ah!

MATRON. And what's more, I'm beginning to feel grateful to you.

MRS. H. What?

MATRON. You forced me to do something I should have done years ago—tell Susan.

MRS. H. Well! Blow me down!

MATRON (*smiling*). So I'll help you finance that clinic you want.

(MRS. H. *stares, open-mouthed.*)

VICCY. Matron! You won't!

MATRON. Oh! I'll only *lend* her the money, and I shall want interest on it, but she *did* help me once, and she has had a bad time in my house, so I owe her something.

VICCY. Well! I'm——

MRS. H. You are being very generous, Emilia. I don't know what to say.

MATRON. Say nothing. I want you to leave in the morning. Everything will be arranged by my solicitors.

MRS. H. (*rising*). You won't regret this. I'll make money and repay you as soon as possible.

MATRON (*firmly*). I expect you to do so. Good night.

MRS. H. (*moving to door*). I feel as though I've had coals of fire heaped on my head! But thank you. Thank you very much. Good night.

(MATRON *and* VICCY *watch her as she exits.*)

MATRON. Get us both a drink, Viccy. I think we need one.

VICCY (*moves to table back and pours drinks*). What an evening!

MATRON. Yes, as you say! What an evening!

(VICCY *brings the drinks and sits on settee.*)

(*As she sips.*) Thank you.

(*Enter* SUSAN.)

SUSAN (*as she enters*). Well, we've settled Mrs. Winstone in bed and Dr. Soames has gven her a sedative.

MATRON. Good.

VICCY (*sipping*). Let me finish this and I'm off.

MATRON. No, don't go, Viccy. I think we should clear one or two things up.

(SUSAN *sits at desk.*)

VICCY. Yes?

MATRON. Firstly, I have decided to make this clinic into a company and to give both you and Susan a substantial interest in it.

SUSAN. But Aunt——

MATRON. Please listen, Sue. I know you want to marry Hugh Barrett, but that little cottage of his isn't far from here. You could still be my secretary, couldn't you?

SUSAN (*springing up, her face radiant*). Aunt!— Does this mean?——

MATRON. Yes. I realize now that I've grown into such an acidulated old spinster that I'd forgotten almost what it was like to be in love. Tonight—I remembered.

SUSAN (*kneeling near her*). I don't know what to say! But of course I can still help you. I never wanted to desert you. Oh, Aunt! It will be wonderful. (*She turns to* VICCY.) Won't it, Viccy?

VICCY. Yes, Sue, wonderful.

MATRON. Then don't you think you had better ring Mr. Barrett? I understand from Milly that he has been haunting the stables all day.

SUSAN. What?

MATRON. —Looking extremely miserable! I can't have him upsetting the horses, you know.

SUSAN. Oh! Aunt!

VICCY. Go on. Put the poor boy out of his misery.

SUSAN (*picking up telephone*). I'll just tell him that I'll meet him tomorrow.

MATRON. Yes—and ask him to dinner.

SUSAN (*very happily*). Yes, Aunt. (*Into telephone.*) I want Shelford double three five—yes, double three five.

(*As she waits,* MATRON *and* VICCY *talk.*)

MATRON. You haven't said anything about my offer, Viccy?

VICCY (*uneasily*). No—I don't know quite what to say. You see, I'd decided to leave here.

MATRON. Oh! No, Viccy! Not now. I've so many plans. I couldn't do without you.

SUSAN (*into telephone*). Is that you, Hugh? Yes. It's Sue. (*There is a long pause. Her face is radiant as she listens.*) Yes, darling. . . . Yes, everything is all right. . . . Of course I will. . . . Yes, darling, soon . . . very soon.

(*The rest of the conversation is spoken softly and we hear* VICCY *and* MATRON *talking above her voice.*)

So was I . . . very miserable. . . . Oh! you poor darling. . . . Yes, tomorrow, as soon as I can. . . . Yes, about ten. . . . Oh! Aunt says will you come to dinner tomorrow night. . . . Yes, she *did*. . . . Isn't it wonderful!

(*She goes babbling on until she hangs up.*)

VICCY (*to* MATRON, *ignoring* SUSAN). Plans? What plans?

MATRON. I want to expand this place. I think it's time we opened a male clinic.

VICCY. What?

MATRON. Men are as figure-conscious as women these days. Well? What do you say?

VICCY. A male clinic! Now that might be interesting.

MATRON. Interesting, *and*, I think, profitable. Well?— Are you going to stay and help me?

VICCY (*slowly*). Men here! Now that's certainly something.

MATRON (*impatiently*). Viccy, are you staying?

VICCY. I *am*—I most certainly *am*. (*She laughs.*)

MATRON Then you must see these plans.

(*She moves the desk. As she reaches it,* SUSAN *puts down telephone. She still has a bemused look of happiness on her face.*)

(*Softly.*) Is everything all right now?

SUSAN. Yes—oh, yes— Everything is wonderful, Aunt, wonderful.

VICCY (*to* SUE). Did you hear all that? No, of course you didn't. But I think you may be right—everything is wonderful!

SUSAN (*happily*). Of course it is!

VICCY (*whirling round the stage*). No more the "dim and dedicated spinsterhood" for *you*—my pet—and I think—not for me— *Men!*——
(*They both laugh.*)

THE CURTAIN FALLS.

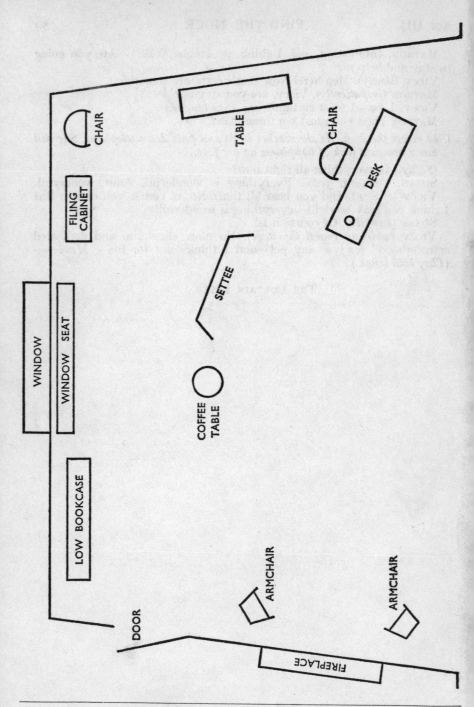